To Ken Bezar

Enjoy your Moments

SUDDEN MUSIC

Endo Quest 2002

Ed Carlson

sudden music

IMPROVISATION, SOUND, NATURE

David Rothenberg

THE UNIVERSITY OF GEORGIA PRESS

ATHENS

Published by the University of Georgia Press

Athens, Georgia 30602

© 2002 by David Rothenberg

All rights reserved

Designed by Erin Kirk New

Set in 10.5 on 15 Minion by G & S Typesetters

Printed and bound by Thomson-Shore

The paper in this book meets the guidelines for permanence
and durability of the Committee on Production Guidelines
for Book Longevity of the Council on Library Resources.

Printed in the United States of America

06   05   04   03   02   C   5   4   3   2   1

Library of Congress Cataloging-in-Publication Data

Rothenberg, David, 1962–

Sudden music : improvisation, sound, nature / David Rothenberg.

    p. cm.

Discography: p.

Includes bibliographical references (p.).

ISBN 0-8203-2318-7 (alk. paper)

1. Music—Philosophy and aesthetics. 2. Improvisation (Music)

3. Nature (Aesthetics) I. Title.

ML3877 .R68 2002

781.3′6 — dc21   2001027721

FOR IVAN

CONTENTS

SUDDEN MUSIC

The wind breathes in from the window, sending paper swirling in the room. The trees are bent, leaves blow down. There is no particular pattern to this movement, except that each year it happens around the same time. Although the forces of nature seem to work in cycles, they do not decide things and then act them out. Rather, they play with rules they can't escape, providing endless variation that still lies within a plan. These are the best kind of plans to have: those that allow sudden surprises that you never tire of, without ending in lives of total chaos.

This is a book about improvisation, in music, life, and nature. It is not meant to be a method for how to live spontaneously or how to create in the moment. No, it is more about seeing the world as a confluence of sudden happenings, where the order we discover emerges as the result of chance. This book is an account of incidents that have led me to create, or that convinced me that sudden music is the most beautiful music, both literally as something to play and figuratively as a way to hear the whole world as a musical happening, making each step forward a musical gesture, a part in the song of the world.

The poet and the improviser alike look for connections among things so seemingly incongruous that at first contact they seem to make no sense. A black crow on white snow. A dead convertible in the mud flats. A centipede dashing out of the floppy drive. A blossom in the cement. Their impulse is to find meaning everywhere, in everything from the smallest coincidence to the greatest mistake. The improviser does not dwell on any one decision before seeking openly to find the next. The method may not generate any result of deep or great structure. But it keeps one's attentiveness alive.

I write as a musician, ecologist, and philosopher, trying to speak with some authority on the ways these roles fit together and each vantage point informs the other. I cannot plan the linkages of these worlds. They sometimes simply happen. Often they pass each other aimlessly at night.

I want to create a musical path into the richly present rhythms of the world. It is difficult to explain or map out. The confusion of the world rages on past the fading away of a lone person's easy routes through it. The musical moment is one that captures ambiguity, rather than reducing reality to an easy chord. We do not know the universe any better if we imagine that even the unexpected happenings can be somehow contained within rules. We are better off when we know just where the rules stop, and where we are left to sudden invention given the very little that we are ever able to know. There is no preparation for the improvising life besides learning glimmers of the background rules and not being afraid to bend them to fit the changing situation. I would not say push and pull the rules a bit so as to stay in a game that continually evolves. No, this is not a plea for moderation. The interesting life is not always a balanced life. Take risks for their sake alone.

It is easy to find this urgency when you're moving around, trying to figure out why you cannot keep still. The tourist, wrote Paul Bowles in *The Sheltering Sky,* has a planned itinerary, a fixed vacation, and knows where and how long he will be gone. The *traveler,* in contrast, has absolutely no idea where he is going, how long it will take, or when, if ever, he will return.

This book is a recital of travels: musical, natural; some specific, others general. It is a guide for the perplexed in me, and hopefully for the uncertainties in you, too. How do we maintain the joys of spontaneity and sudden creativity when there is so much we are told we have to accomplish? Life is supposed to have a beginning, middle, and end, and yet we strive to create works that will last forever, to contribute to culture and the world in a way that will last beyond our brief lifetimes. What results is never what we planned. How can we make the most of this doubt?

My aim is to build on my experience as an improviser—in music, in listening to the world—to suggest that there is a way to learn from suddenness to make the most out of a life. If we are able to respond nimbly to situations, sounds, and changes in direction that cannot be foreseen, we will know what to practice. Listen to the voices around you that are not your own, and learn when to play and when to sit one out.

Hold on to connections between things; when they surprise you, think about why you didn't expect things to come together just there. When a chance encounter—whether between people, places, ideas, or opposites that don't want to attract—seems way beyond the odds, hold on to it, realize you've just beaten the system. This is the way the world works. Chance favors all of us if we know when to accept it. The trick is to decide which such encounters are worth remembering, transformed into art. You want to become the thread that weaves through all that fraying real fabric. That is your story, your song.

Take two sounds that have nothing at all to do with one another: an eagle's cry and a passing train; the screech of chalk on a blackboard and a major chord. Figure out how to build a piece that makes use of both.

Don't plan it out, just go. This is improvisation—it will happen without the studied plan. You constantly train for it, and then you're ready. To hear, to see, to bring the disparate and far-flung together in an instant you've prepared for all your life: this is improvisation.

Pick any two places, with nothing in common save that you have been there. Jumbesi, Nepal? Iona, Scotland? Layer them upon each other, and listen. What sort of music do you hear? This will be your melody, your strand.

When I was twenty years old I spent some months living in Nepal, a semester away from the confines of a college education. Unsure what to do once I got there, I decided, after hanging around the exiled Tibetan Buddhist monasteries at the eastern edge of Katmandu, to investigate some of the distant details of Tibetan music. As a clarinetist, I was intrigued with the Tibetan wind instrument the *gyaling,* a conical-bored instrument with a double reed that is always played in pairs. Repeating seemingly endless meandering melodies, players breathe quickly in through the nose as they continue the flow of air into the instrument, allowing a continuous sound that has no need ever to stop: a technique known as circular breathing.

Like any unfamiliar music, the tunes of the gyaling at first sounded all alike to my untrained ear. Only with careful study did I come to hear distinct melodic differences. All the music was made out of material covering less than one octave, only six notes. But that was enough. We choose our constraints, as Stravinsky said, to allow the greatest freedom of expression. Set the rules—then play among them.

As a diligent expatriate student, I had set the bounds of my inquiry. I now proceeded to find out as much as I could about this one instrument and its one kind of music. I walked for days to visit Lama Sangye Tenzin in the monastery at Jumbesi for help on this quest. While he discoursed on enlightenment I pestered him about the curious gyaling, this gaudy, decorated oboesque thing whose name even means "horn from a strange place." What could he tell me about it? He laughed under his breath. I knew what he was thinking: What could this young American, with his peculiar and specialized questions, want? Why learn about the gyaling apart from the entire tradition of our life here? He looked up and answered: "The music is but one part of our whole world. It makes no sense taken away from that world. Why do you care so much about this one strange thing?"

That's what they teach us to do back home, I thought. To reduce a problem to small enough pieces that it becomes something we can tackle. At the end we try to fit the whole together again out of all the pieces. But I didn't want to tell him that. Instead, I improvised: "Think of the gyaling as a window. A frame from something somewhat familiar to me. I am a musician. I play the winds. We blow into them, put our fingers on the holes, and sound comes out. From this experience, through this glass, I can gaze just a bit onto your culture, a place very different from mine, and perhaps catch a glimpse of something much more important, something that might take a lifetime to understand. Please do not laugh at my questions. Take them as an innocent place to begin."

Ah, perhaps I wished I had said that, or would have said that now. Then, I sat silently, probably knowing I deserved to be laughed at. How dare we imagine we can travel somewhere far away and learn enough of something far off and distant in so short a time, then come back home and expound on what we found out. Each contact between one culture and another is a sudden meeting of distant worlds. We become specialists at inventing stories of the global village, tales that have no proper place except around the campfires of the journey, in the conversations of those who know that the world is an open place where each can partake of so much while never entirely managing to settle in, always needing to move on in order to make the most of any experience or possibility.

Tenzin soon found a way not to laugh at my interest. "Sure," he said to me in a Nepali simple enough for me to grasp, big Tibetan-English and English-Sanskrit dictionaries covering the table between us. "This music can be a way into the tradition. In any one piece lies the whole meaning of our study here. Take this melody" —he demonstrates on a *lingbu,* an easy-to-play flute, like a recorder. "You could play the whole thing, beginning to end, in several minutes. Or you could draw it out, adding ornaments, warbling trills, moving more slowly from one pattern to another, repeating a few longer, getting the most out of each change, inhabiting the music as far as you can go, and it could take"—he paused to consider—"thirteen hours. Or thirteen years even. That is the amount of time students stay with us to learn the fundamentals of our way of life. Then they return to their homes, and their changing lives. Of course," and he sipped a bit more of his salty butter tea, "you will be with us only for a short while, and must learn what you can."

"Is the longer piece necessarily the deeper one?" I asked.

"You need time," reflected Tenzin, "to get a sense of the meaning of what happens."

I taped all our conversations. Today when I listen to them I am amazed to hear myself speaking coherent phrases in a language I no longer understand. It has all faded away into myth and story. I remember clearly, though, hearing patterns and warblings repeating endlessly, all sounding the same, just like one another, no differentiation, and then how, after learning the foreign and otherworldly logic, I began to hear subtle differences in each, minute changes that I soon perceived as momentous, because the range of notes is so limited. Rules are followed exactly, and then, almost miraculously, they are broken, for a split second, with ease. Permanence, and then impermanence. Just when you think you understand the system it stands on its head.

How much of the surprise is known in advance? How much of it is improvisation, twisted in and around the moment, based on rules, but bending the rules? Tenzin and I understood each other, I believed. We both saw tradition as important, but not fixed. It evolves precisely through encounters such as ours. At the same time, even as I sought spontaneity, I wanted think. Tibetan melodies have no conventional notation, though sometimes the low, deep chants, now well known in the West, are noted in the sacred texts with a swirly, florid roll of the pen, like medieval European neumes. But melodies, why write these down? wondered the Master. Aren't they best as living sound, passed from one musician to another.

Legitimacy, I offered. In my country, it must be on paper or it is not legitimate, fixed, possibly eternal, lasting at least until the document yellows and crumbles.

That's what I said, but I didn't really believe it. Music is fluid, vital. For it to continue to live it cannot be frozen on the page.

Well why not try and write down your melodies anyway, I suggested. Let's see where they go. And so he disappeared for a day and returned with a cryptic squiggly line, the first recorded instance of the notation of a Tibetan melody in a native way:

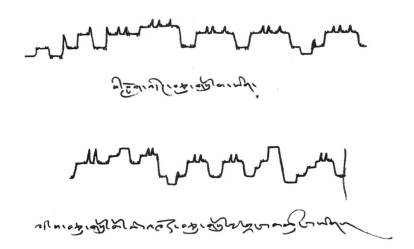

The caption reads, in Tibetan script: "The thirteen chapters of the piece Se Lo, each symbolizing one of the thirteen levels in the study of the Dharma." Drawn between November 15 and 18, 1982, by Sangye Tenzin Lama in Jumbesi, Nepal.

The music flutters eloquently and endlessly: there are no breaks in the sound as the gyaling players use circular breathing to transcend breath, to blow forever. I can finish the piece in a minute or a lifetime, depending on how much I hear and experiment with it. In each case it is the same piece of music, heard across a different range.

It has been said that the music of the gyaling is what one would hear inside one's own mind if all other sounds were to be shut out. The more you choose to inhabit this world of sound, the more present the unending tones will be. I still hear them today, eighteen years after I heard them for the first time. But then, perhaps I have endeavored to keep the rhythms in me as part of the search either for permanence or for something truly worth remembering out of the flow of time. In a minute or in a lifetime I want something that can be called *the same.*

The piece of music is but a small part of another world, a window onto larger things. At the same time it is a record, a symbol for the whole itself. The whole world in a blade of grass, the ocean in a dewdrop. It takes work to learn to hear these things. Knowing the beginning and end of a piece of this music is not as important as knowing the full range of possible variations that could occur at any moment and having the patience and decisiveness to choose just one, knowing as well that next time you might choose something very different. But never is everything permitted. Nebulous bounds always apply, always constrain.

I am no longer so concerned with writing the music down. Today I want to play whatever can't be written down. But at the same time, I want to be free from history so I can weave my own account out of the already faded cloth of memories, ancient and recent. I still want to remember what has happened, and I'll use words and pictures there in addition to any recollection I retain of the original sound.

One day the monastery was preparing for a great *puja* that would last several days, running all through the nights, and the whole orchestra would be gathered to invoke the gods and send music thundering across the hillsides for the duration. I knew this would be a tumultuous and total experience, one that I thought I should share with someone, someone from my world, or at least from the world outside. So I went down the to the small teahouse in the village at the base of the hill, frequented by trekkers on the long march to the area around Mount Everest. A young man walked in, gaunt, as haggard as the rest of us who were subsisting on potatoes, tea, and *tsampa,* with the usual scraggly beard. He was on his way, but from no particular place to any other. A perfect candidate. I told him about the impending festivities at the monastery on the hill. "You ought to come," I suggested. His plans were open.

That night the musicians were gathered, everyone in their places.

We guests, having been made welcome, sat off to the side, taking in the festivities. The monks, most of them under fifteen years of age, wore maroon robes and yellow hats. The *tankga* paintings were unfurled, the freshly printed prayer flags strewn about the hall. The chants began through the texts: the lama would intone or mumble for a while, and eventually the young monks would join in, chanting in rhythm, "da *da* da da da da da *da* da da da da," then breaking for a clash of cymbals and gyaling strains, punctuated with rattles and drums, all in a gnash of demons and deities running and screaming as we called upon the spirits to enliven the proceedings.

A platter of ornate foods was passed around, strange confections that I can barely remember, only that their colors were bizarre and bright. I leaned over to my new friend, whose name I don't think I ever learned. "Careful," I told him. "This food is . . . "

Let's freeze the story right there. Now, two years later I was on the island of Iona in Scotland, and the music of Nepal was in the far recesses of my mind. Iona is the famous destination of spiritual pilgrimage in the Western Isles, where the gospel first came to Scotland from Ireland with a few intrepid monks many, many years ago. Today all sorts of spiritual wanderers come there, to stay and work at the monastery and participate in ecumenical services and practices. I heard there a sermon invoking Gandhi, Martin Luther King, and the Dalai Lama all somehow as part of Christian tradition. The water was an immediate dark blue and the wind was bristling and clear.

Everyone who had joined the community, most just for the summer season, was on some sort of quest for a goal they could not quite articulate. I started a conversation with the organist, an Australian named Michael Havir who had a knack for combining musical elements from many traditions the same way the minister was blending exemplary figures in the pulpit. Like many Australians, he had been traveling for years. "Costs so much to leave down under," he said; "might as well stay away while we can." He too had been in Nepal, around the same time I was there. We shared our perplexities about the place: "Wasn't it strange that the whole country declared a holiday the day Brezhnev died?" "Did you run into Robert Redford trekking beneath Everest as well? The brooding young Austrian obsessed with obtaining a snow leopard pelt?" He'd seen all these people, too. We'd covered each other's tracks, all around the same time. "Yes," he reminisced. "I remember being in one little village and meeting a scruffy young American who invited me up to a ceremony at his monastery. There were all kinds of sounds, a terrible din really, but huge plates of ornate foods. I was about to reach over and stuff my hungry face with some of this stuff, and he stopped me and said. . . ."

"Careful, this food is only *marginally safe*," I finished the sentence effortlessly, realizing it was me he was talking about! He was the traveler I had found by chance in the village two years before. Now we had met again, thousands of miles away. For no reason. That's just the way it was. We couldn't even recognize each other because our appearances, at least, had recovered since the Himalaya. Those mountains hollow you out, take twenty pounds off you, reduce you to an outline, gaunt, all the fat and excess washed away. Unshaven, unwashed for weeks, in fraying clothes, the Himalayan traveler pursues sketchy paths and aimless wanderings. You meet someone on the trail, and you expect never to see them again. But even random ramblings cross time and time again.

There is little obvious connection between a far-off Sherpa monastery and the pilgrimage site of Iona Isle—except that both are spiritual destinations. A certain kind of seeker tends to end up in such a place, even if the journey is never exactly planned. I hesitate to call myself a seeker, even though I oft find myself in such places. I never expect to find any answers there, though the suspicion always exists within me that there is more in this world than there appears to be. Even on improbable journeys, we are not alone.

Since that time I've tried to keep track of Mike. For a few years he lived in London. I don't remember what odd jobs he was up to, but I know that for a while he was obsessed with finding a natural way to stop wearing glasses. He rigorously practiced the optometric exercises popularized by Aldous Huxley, where one simply refuses to wear glasses and becomes used to the blurriness of the nearsighted world. Trace the fuzzy outlines of things with your misshapen eyes until the objects' clarity comes through, transcending the imperfect information brought in by your senses. Michael's resolve was impressive. He got used to walking around not really being able to see.

Perhaps a blurred vision encourages imagination to fill in the blanks. Like when you walk a week in the mountains with someone who does not speak your language, but you know you are together and there is a reason for the trip and you will make it together and share something of the walk. You both will return home, though you may meet again, on the other side of the world. Perhaps you will then be speaking different languages and will be hard-pressed to remember anything about the other except the strangeness of one encounter, and then a second, and maybe hope for another.

I decided it was important to remain aware of Mike, wherever we ended up. He went back to Australia, surfacing as the only white guy in the Aboriginal pop band Yothu Yindi, who went to number one in Sydney with their song "Treaty Yeah." Mike played the keyboards. They played at the United Nations on International Indigenous Peoples Day. The band traveled the world. Then I lost track of him: when my list of far-flung friends was computerized, somehow his name didn't make it. I search for him from time to time on the Internet, but with no results. Just as well; if I found him and we reconnected, the meeting would not be as random as before. The world is now like this.

Why does this story matter? Coincidence is legion, we all touch it once in a while. "I met the same traveler again years later. . . ." So what?

For me, the mere possibility of such a meeting holds hope. Chance *can* matter. Accidental meaning is essential for improvisation, because we are never fully in control. When we don't know where the order of the work is coming from, wonderful surprises can result. The stories that matter most, which are often never written down, evolve and recombine in memory so thoroughly that the truth becomes hard after a generation to pin down.

Some fear that if they improvise friendships there will be no order to their life. Some find that these unplanned meetings and partings leave one very much alone. But plans in so complex a world are difficult to fulfill. If you can find meaning in chance encounter, you will be very lucky, because there are so many such encounters in the sea of information, the placeless world we run from but still run in.

Think about this too much, though, and you risk losing the surprise. Travel is transformed in stories, and the suddenness soon becomes fixed. Beware of turning your experience into anecdotes, the same stories you'll tell everyone. And refrain from making yourself the hero in these stories. Similar things happen to all of us—always listen more than you tell, take in more than you dish out, arrive at more places than you leave.

Think of the encounters that could have happened, the friends streaming by on an opposite track, that glimmer of recognition as the familiar car turns a corner, a ready memory but far out of place. Most of the connections, we miss. Most of the meaning, we have never seen. Someone who could have mattered so much to you was walking two streets away, parallel, going in the same direction, but you will never find her. Perhaps she is on her way to the same place you are, yet you cannot share the walk. Then twenty years later she is behind you on the highway, with an important message, and you won't get it because you turn off one exit too soon.

Alone on a rock by the side of a river, on the phone forty stories up in the fog, we fail to connect. The line is busy, the machines have all stopped, we've been around the world and come back to the same room. No one has missed us, the world has gone on. This is still no time to make plans. Leave again, ready to be open to the unknown. Out the door: right or left? There is no sure way to decide.

These random meetings of two players adrift in the world form a ceaseless, inaudible music that lies usually unheard. Neither player is important in any sense of the world's turnings, but what better way to become significant than to keep track of accident, to weigh down the lightness of encounters so that the sudden stories will become more continuous. These places—America, the Himalaya, Scotland, Australia—are impossible to share in any single musical moment, for we move among them. There are overlapping melodies. There is one single chord. We inhabit it with meaning. We forget all those other connections that never even happened. This is the real memory. This is what we will hold and sing.

What kind of music results from a chance encounter, from the unplanned meeting of two minds, two styles, two structures in sound put forth by people who know nothing of one another and are never sure what will result. Try it once. Try it again, ten years later, with the same person. Hear what you each have learned. How many meetings are necessary to create a shared history? How much can we remember of an instant collective sound?

Human wandering is rarely aimless. We follow scents, whiffs, encouragement, and meet people with similar goals. Natural, isn't it? When I checked out three century-old books from the Widener Library and noticed that the same person had checked them all out together in 1908, I wondered: Who was that man? Ought I try to find out? No one would reveal to me such privileged information. If I discover the man's identity it means I was taught to persevere.

By pushing unrelated things against each other, toward some remarkable and necessary effect, disparate words can be made to belong together. The same ideas travel through so many writers' words, meeting each other with shock again and again. You might cut them out, collect them, paste them into some new form.

A few years ago the Canadian Centre for Architecture in Montreal asked me to perform a musical piece on the theme of "constructed space" for a gathering they were arranging. Actually, they first asked me to speak, but I would always rather play than talk. I came up with a piece mixing music and spoken words.

Begin your improvised music with a single word. Say, "antelope" or "cemetery." "Threadbare" or "swoon." Make up a line of phrases, play until the suggestiveness of the word has run its course. Then, as you're finishing your part, assess it as it winds down. Decide how you've made out. Stop the music, take a breath, end with another word, one that suddenly describes where you've been. What is it? "Zoo," "deathbed," "frayed," "seduced"? This is one way music finds its way through words.

The words in the piece I performed in Canada came from several sources. I began with an inspiration from urban theorist Jane Jacobs, who believes that the chance encounter underlies the best in urban life: you never know whom you might meet, right in front of your own door. Then I remembered that the poet Wallace Stevens once said that "French and English are the same language," obviously a contentious thing to bring up in Montreal. Stevens was also an executive in the insurance industry. Although he always claimed that his essays on the insurance of buildings against damage from fire had nothing to do with his poems, I felt they sounded very much alike. In his guarded reticence runs something of the schizophrenic ravings of the dancer Vaslav Nijinsky, losing control of his life as he journeyed through the mountains to the self, writing it all down because it was what he had to do to maintain some glimmer of sanity. Then Reb Nachman of Bratslav, that mystical eighteenth-century Hasidic rebbe whose tales seem so timeless and unpedagogical, tries to point a way from individual observation and testimony out to the world as a whole. It's all held together by a thread of chance, like a walk down a city street, when you're trying to get where you need to be and at the same time take everything in, to be open to all possible influences, senses, sounds, smells. If you manage to be so open you might well lose your way. But we are alive to *taste* as much of life as we dare.

Here I'm talking about the music without mentioning the music. Phrases roll out so easily when their subject is language, not the ambiguous throom that pure sound may offer. But use words musically, and you will eventually need them no more. Either every sound will be explained, or you will give up the whole task of explaining.

"It all starts with a walk down a street," Jane Jacobs says. I spread out her words and find an analytic, spoken poetry in them (all to be heard over undulating, strange sounds made familiar by their easy rhythm).

> The sight of people still attracts other people.
> The gaze returns still other gazes.
> The stillness demands activity.
> The planners of the city think that city people
> seek the sight of emptiness, obvious order and quiet.
> Nothing could be less true.

A street has its users and its watchers: there are those walking unconsciously through the path of sound; those taking notes on the sidelines. There are those caught in between these tasks, documenting the place, creating their role by writing. The city offers us the strange. There is no need to travel. It's all right here. *Who believes that? Those who are incessantly roaming in search of yet more unplanned encounters that will gravitate toward meaning over the years?* Surprise meetings in the city can make you feel like you are roving all over the globe. Why, in New York it can be as likely to meet a friend from Helsinki as from the other side of town. Everyone is always passing through. That's how a sensible identity is crafted out of all those possible encounters.

But the diagram of the sensible is always capable of unraveling toward the senseless. Nijinsky saw the value of wandering only after he was no longer fully in control. Half mad, and the words just flew out of him:

Once in the mountains I came to a road which led up to a peak.
I climbed up and stopped.
I wanted to make a speech on the mountain;
I felt a wish to do so, but I did not because
I thought that everyone would say I was mad.
I was not. I had a great wish to speak.
I felt no pain, but a great love toward the people.
I wanted to shout from the mountain into the village of St. Moritz.
I did not because I felt I had to continue my way.
I went on and came to a tree.
The tree told me that one could not talk here,
because *human beings do not understand feeling.*
I was sorry to part with the tree, because the tree understood me.

He is roaming through the landscape, wishing only to express himself. Nature may be the ideal listener, or it may be a blank slate. Human beings may not understand feeling, but at least we do feel. We notice. We are influenced, bent, moved, even when we don't know why. Yet many of us have talked to trees, especially at hours of need. They are stable, magnanimous; in place for years. How do we pick which one matters for us? From a chance glance, or after years watching the rustling of leaves? But Nijinsky gets more out of the tree: he gets a plea for silence. The leaves want no words. They don't want us. Nature goes on without question, without speculation. Yet it has built so much—all, as we are told to believe, by way of chance.

Why are the testaments of a great artist at his personal lowest so interesting? It takes a fall to push the dancer to write. It is not his true medium, but he needs to make his descent explicit. The world of art becomes too much, and the raving walk through the forests is an obvious therapy. Moving from incident to incident, whatever appears, there is a multitude to talk about. A great artist makes a sensible madman.

Walking on through the city streets, glancing down at your feet, looking for meaning in the magic and technical markings of the reconstructed city being built all around us. There is no harm in interpreting a sign that was not put there for you. The reader *reads* whatever catches her glance, the musician hears song where others are making noise, the artist sees a palette of colors in steel gray sky.

Wallace Stevens's lectures on insurance display the same wry dance between sense and absurdity characteristic of his poetry. I suspect that even in his business he lived poetically, following whatever links his imagination offered him, completing thoughts equally with flights of fancy and with fact.

> Truth is, we may well be entering an insurance era. Compare the man who insures his dwelling against fire with that personality of the first plane who, at a stroke, insures all dwellings against fire and who, without stopping to think about it, insures not only the lives of all those that live in the dwellings, but insures all people against all happenings

of everyday life, even the worm in the apple or the piano out of tune. There is no difference between the worm in the apple and the tack in the can of sardines, and not the slightest difference between the piano out of tune and the person disabled.

No difference? Only in poetry, not insurance. The expansion from the one case to all cases is the leap of generalization, what we're warned not to do, why philosophy always fails and we're supposed to trust our *guts* to figure out how to act in any sudden situation, musical or otherwise, at home or abroad, indoors or out, on itinerary or with many days lost. Yet who doesn't want to announce meaning from a sudden realization, an accidental juxtaposition of one idea upon another? We want that wonderful moment of insight to last! *We* want to last so much longer than our flicker on this earth, or than the instant when everything seems clear, that instant that so immediately slips away.

Disabled, and then enabled. Somewhere off key, discovering your own, possibly dangerous, voice. You may express things more clearly than ever, but this doesn't mean you will escape danger in life, in passing from one day to the next.

To be safe, insure it all. Claim it all. Reach as far as you dare and prepare for the worst. But there is no insurance against missed opportunity, failing to meet that stranger two years later on another continent thousands of miles away. What if you arrived a day late or early? Or stayed comfortably in the next room? The only thing to stay sad about is about how much possible experience we all have missed.

This is why one instance can be made to stand for many. Why we easily learn from what has happened to others. We are not so different; stories seldom are all new. Reb Nachman has no lessons to impart to us over the centuries, but rather images, cyclical stories, fantastical journeys with ends that have nothing at all to do with

their beginnings. He too wants to fill the world from a moment—
this time, with a moment's laugh:

> Among all countries there is one country
> which includes all countries
> (in that it serves as the rule for all countries).
> In that country there is one city
> which includes all cities
> of the whole country
> which includes all countries.
> In that city there is a house which
> includes all the houses which
> includes all the cities of the country
> which includes all countries.
>
> And there is a man who includes everybody
> from that house which
> includes all the houses which
> includes all the cities of the country
> which includes all countries.
>
> And that man knows all the jokes of the country,
> and of all the countries in the world.

I'm not sure if the story is funny or not. If you truly are able to laugh
everywhere, just where, then, is your home?

They tell me I come from an uprooted people. Among these people,
as the stories go, were many pious men, rebbes left and right working miracles in the old country and the new. Ah, but I cannot identify with that. Music and the earth are my games. Incessant belief
and exact rules have always given me trouble.

The musicians of the rebbe's court at Sanz, home of my direct
ancestors, were known throughout the old country, in Galicia and

beyond. Their talent at celebrating devotion was unmatched, mark my words. This following fact seems of interest, right here, right now: This rebbe insisted that his musicians use no music that had been written down. He had that, at least, in common with Lama Sangye Tenzin. "Such music," the rebbe said, "is as dead as frozen thoughts trapped in words. Music that lives cannot be caught, it always eludes capture."

This book is not about how to hear or to make music. It may be about how to *be* music, how to sense music as an essential presence in this and any other place we may find ourselves. Nor is it about any one kind of music over any other. In fact, when the word *music* appears, you will often have to fill in the blank with *your* music —what you play, what you choose to hear, what you hear wafting through doors and windows you are powerless to close. We wait for it, we learn it, we entice it, we become it.

There is a nasty tendency to get lost in abstract questions when all you ever want is one concrete answer, one example to frame the endless quest. As Reb Nachman suggests, the great encompassing plan only laughs at itself in the end. He wants an ideal Platonic country, and all he gets is a smile.

How hard it is to write about music, to substitute for sounds specific words that the world of sounds so gracefully elides! This is why music criticism is often so hollow, because writers are forced to make out of music an argument, to take the ineffable and alogical and imagine it stands for something. Do the titles of instrumental pieces help give them meaning, or do they distract us from the pieces' lack of meaning?

Among musics there ought to be a way to play that encompasses all other ways. Not so much to make all of them unnecessary, but to surround them with a smile. Improvisation makes waves through traditions, and any tradition that endures long enough should allow for spontaneous creativity within it. Any sound played convincingly should admit the possibility of travel, that it could easily move from one musical world to another and make sense through surprising contacts, resonances, along the way.

Place two radios next to one another, each tuned to a different station. Pick two styles of music that barely relate. Close your eyes, listen to both, try to find a third sense between the two and play along in that vein. Then stop the music. Keep the two sources ringing inside your head—remember the odd juxtaposition. Let your imagination hold on to that thought. Hear the guides in yourself that no one else can hear. Then begin, again, to play.

Chaos, order, movement from the unprecedented to the unexpected, but a twist, if not familiar, then acceptable: like Bach bending the rules to write magic in the tradition, not mere formality. I have spoken of the chance encounter, one that can take place anywhere, anywhere here in the world. I want to make it matter *more*, to nurture delight at the strange coincidences that bring people together, and the music that comes when you fold one unrelated story in and around another. Only the traveler that has both stories in mind holds them both in common. Traveler, not tourist. Always lost, but never off schedule.

There remains a danger. What if no one else can follow, no one else sees the path between these same things? So often we travel so fast, miles high in the air. If you choose to gaze down on the real world, as at a map, you may see places that you once have touched with your feet. Once, flying over a familiar mountainous landscape, I felt this tactile knowledge, but with it came a well of sadness. My journey of raw encounters had been made too much alone. I had climbed all those mountains, but with many different others. Who else remembered the journeys? When I met them again years later, they had forgotten where we had been. Here's what I wrote of this feeling:

You can trace the masks of dwelling by air
Back above the continent, I gaze down at mountains I have known,
as the high plane curves in from unending oceans
First over Gaspé: Jacques Cartier, into Maine:
Katahdin, Cadillac, Bigelow, then the Whites:
Jefferson, Cardigan, Moosilauke on down
to monadnocks alone: Greylock, Overlook, Peekamoose,
then the wide swerve to the ground.

I remember the routes
and can trace the trails
even from thirty thousand feet—

There is no comfort in knowing this terrain
As each path I have climbed was with someone else
at the base camps I returned alone.
There is no bridge from one peak to the next
each ascent leads eventually nowhere.

Life then a sequence of walls climbed and unclimbed
each trip just back to where it began,
no journey taken to prove a thing.

Of a wandering people,
I still want a pattern from one trail to the next
and there is nothing but valleys or clouds.

Now, how can that pattern be made musically? My problem is
that I don't want to play anything that has already been played before. Although I am not interested in fitting in, I do want music to
help me find a home in the world. To improvise, you train for the
unexpected, holding inside you a slew of possibilities that you cannot forget once you've made your choice of rhythms and notes.
Hear everything else that is not played as you play!

I want to be both my unique traveling self and have a true place
to come back to. Who doesn't want that? We're trained to be ever

original, yet so much has already been done. That is why the temptation exists to meander through all these previous happenings. We crave the validation of the chance encounter that so suddenly can give sense to the aimlessness of movement itself. Improvisation makes sense when any accord or dissonance seems to fit within the whole. Life does it when the accidental proves to be necessary and more luminous than the path that was planned. Jumbesi, Iona, Montreal, any crowded street, any mountain that seems to rise on the horizon but in fact is only a heavy cloud—which is the place to belong? The walk from one to another is the self-defining path.

What's the difference between moving between places and bouncing through ideas? Both offer the chance engagement, a link from one text to another, a sketch of the line that connects the dots. We are all looking for our own footprints in the sand, or to find our own thread stitching a special pattern through the fabric that fills the space between the rarest insights. That's right, bend your metaphors so far out of shape that they split at the seams or in between. We're lost, we're on the move, there's no way to stop, there's no map, there's no territory, there's only the screaming song in the world that never ends and has yet to begin. It's always one page beyond that you lose your place, never quite here, impossible to find again until you meet your traveler years later at the other end of the world, in a place that seems strangely familiar, one day to be your home.

Move air from the breeze in the trees to a human breath across a bamboo stalk or bearing down on a reed. Take the forces of nature and tame them into sound. Shut out all else. Concentrate on the *one*. Strive for the perfect tone that will render all other tones excessive and unnecessary. Simplify, constantly simplify so your sound will be able to contain the complex in just one breath. Then stop. Then do it again. That's how to make each note matter.

Music begins with the focus of all effort on the single note. From there it drives on to far complexities, endless flurry, but on the single tone it must be grounded, and to that first note it will eventually return.

One teacher in particular taught me to think this way. For some years I studied jazz clarinet with the taciturn master Jimmy Giuffre, once a big-band composer, then a pioneer with small-group, elegant free jazz, always eminently delicate and listenable. I was one of his last students specifically on the clarinet. This instrument—cool, quiet—had fallen out of fashion in the age of the loud and the cutting. But we both still believed in the need to listen for subtlety. He taught me how to concentrate, to focus, to simplify, to leave room. We would meet for instruction in a small basement studio at the New England Conservatory, and I must say I always found the experience frustrating. I would play a single long tone, and Giuffre would shake his head and say, "No, not right. You haven't yet got the *sound.*" He wanted me to make every note matter, to sing like it was the final knell heralding the end of the world, the last gasp of music anyone would hear before time was over. The tone had to be sudden, immediate, essential, impossible to forget. I hadn't yet reached that point.

Giuffre told me how, when he first picked up the clarinet, switching from the saxophone, he started by playing the lowest note, and that note only, for weeks. Then only when he was ready did he move up to the next note, working with just those two for another few weeks. Then one higher, then another, spending a few months deep down at the bottom of the instrument. He gradually worked his way upward, but stopped at the beginning of the second register, just at the place where most screechy jazz clarinetists begin! He went no further, but kept his play in the low throat tones of the instrument. Higher than a D or so, he couldn't accept his own tone.

The notes did not sound important enough to work with. He stuck with those he was sure would sing.

And so I learned to undertake this patient self-examination myself, working long and hard to be satisfied with the depth of my own sound before gradually reaching higher. Trying to stop the squeakiness, delving into the mellowness, the open air. Months repeating the same few notes, trying not to be bored. Years after learning this way I came across this story, which I have adapted from Stephen Nachmanovitch's book *Free Play*:

> Long ago, a new kind of flute was invented in China. A Japanese master musician was taken by the subtle possibilities of expression it offered and brought it back to his home country. He took out the new flute and played one piece at the end of a concert. When done, there was complete silence in the room, so moved was the crowd. Then the oldest listener spoke softly from the back. "That," he said, "was a song of the gods."
>
> The next day, as the master was preparing to leave the village, the townspeople brought to him their brightest young flutist and asked if the master would take him on as a pupil on this strange new flute. He agreed, taking the young player with him on his journey back to his home in the capital.
>
> The teacher assigned to the student one simple tune, on which the young man would practice incessantly. Each time the master would start by nodding with approval, then change his expression along the way. "No," he would shake his head. "Something is not there." The student begged the master to let him try another piece, just once, but the teacher would not relent. "No—something is still lacking."
>
> The student practiced the single melody for months, years, on end. He came to realize he would never make his teacher happy. One night he packed his bags and snuck away from the master. He stayed in the city until his money ran out. He began to drink, behave erratically, feeling an overwhelming sense of failure. Dejected, he retreated to a tiny

hut far away in the countryside not far from his original village. He lived in rags and occasionally gave beginning lessons to the children of the local farmers. He took out the special flute once in a while, but felt no inspiration to play it. This life went on for many years.

One morning there was a knock on his door. The musicians of his village had learned of his presence. That night there was to be a concert, and they all agreed it could not happen without him. Overcoming his sense of shame, he picked up the flute and went along with them.

The concert began, and many musicians played much music on the old kind of flute, but no one played the new. Near the end of the concert his name was called. He stepped onto the stage disheveled, still in his tattered clothes. He put the flute to his lips and played the only tune he knew. At last he had nothing to gain and nothing to lose. When he finished, there was a long silence the likes of which had not been heard in many years. The old man, now very old indeed, called out softly from the back of the room: "The song of the gods is with us once more."

This could be an anecdote for specialization *or* diligence, suggesting that you must learn to do one thing extremely well, living with its practice for many, many private years. At the same time, the story also suggests how hard it is to achieve anything new given the many vast possibilities that people have been fighting through for years, generations, centuries. Every time I played Giuffre an example of some new kind of music I was working on, he would say, "Yeah, that's nice. I did something like that in the fifties." He'd been there before, and was not easily impressed. There is so much variety in the world that we all have to focus. The story tells us to learn our tune with deep devotion, and stay with it. But what happens if you want to remember nothing? You learn to improvise.

Only when your actions seem without consequence can you realize what you actually know. Improvisation solves no problems, rights no wrongs. It is a swift mutation in the scheme of art. It requires complete attention to all that has come before in order to fill in whatever blanks remain and, at the same time, create new space out of thick air. As an improviser you do not need to memorize tunes or melodies, or even retain any bit of artistic information that has been thrust at you. You must simply know enough to carry the crowd when asked to combine and rework your knowledge at a moment's notice. It can take years to understand how to make the complex appear awesomely simple, as Charles Mingus once described improvisation.

Every musical instrument turns us into a different person, extending the creative ideas of the improviser in directions that couldn't be predicted before the new tool was picked up. The music advances when we do things that we don't expect. That's why it's useful to try a new tool every once in a while. That's also why it's necessary to stick with one that's worth sticking to for years. Move upward slowly, one note at a time. Graduate beyond your limitations to the next plateau. Search slowly on.

I think I know what kind of flute the above parable refers to: the *shakuhachi,* invented in China but refined in Japan over centuries of meditative exploration. A single piece of thick bamboo, cut off near the root, carefully cured, and then a precise notch whittled out of its end. Only five holes drilled into its body. Although this suggests a simple scale of only five notes, the flexibility of the blowing edge makes it possible, with all amounts of breath and vibrato, to produce many more notes than you would expect: from the chromatic scale to microtones in between. A bit like the way a violin allows untold variation with four open-tuned strings.

The shakuhachi is the purest tool for the transformation of air into music. It is among the most difficult instruments to learn to play, because it offers so little: so much is required from within the player. As a result, it can be one of the most rewarding instruments to play. Yet for much of its history it was not even considered a musical instrument, but rather a tool for meditation, a device for the inhabitation of the Zen emptiness of wind itself.

So is it used today by people all over the world, inside music and out, inside Buddhism and out, as a device to investigate the power and possibility of the single tone. It has this ability because of its purity and directness, as well as the fact that it is just so hard to get a sound out of the thing! I picked up the shakuhachi because I wanted to return to the taste of Giuffre's commitment to the one, pure tone. Plus, the shakuhachi is an ideal tool for converging one's musical concentration on the simple task of getting out a single, perfect note, based on an understood breath.

Document what happens when you start to learn to play an instrument. Inherit the permanence of beginnings. Don't write down the music, but try to describe the process of learning to make the instrument your own.

With the shakuhachi, I could at first barely make a sound. Each attempt became an aphorism along the road to the purest tone. I puffed on for weeks, making not a noise at all. Finally a pitch came out, a pure, ringing tone made out of the precise angle and pressure between lip and flute, air and bamboo. But then something strange happened: all the objects in the room started shaking. Had the flute's tone caused all this? Later I learned that this was the first earthquake in New Hampshire in about fifty years.

The pure tone released through the bamboo links player and listener through the power of wind. The rigor and exactness of the tradition suggest no variation, just imitation of the ways of the master, yet the flute immediately draws out the uniqueness of the one who plays it. On the shakuhachi, no two players can or will sound alike. By connecting through sound to the world around, the player finds individuality. Meanwhile, the attention of the listener constantly shifts to immediate sounds; the world around sparkles and crackles, as in the period right after an ear cleaning when the hidden clarity is once again apparent.

Each day I pull out the shakuhachi. It sits by the computer and all the black-box synthesizers, the digital tools of modern music that I tinker with the rest of the time. The flute is the antithesis to all this gadgetry: a single tube of bamboo, only five holes. It survives, penetrating the modern world. There is so much that only the flute, a direct conduit between breath and sound, can do: the bending of tones, the full range of variation. All within, all inside. There are rules, but the rules exist to train a special kind of regimented originality, or discovery of a path that has always been there but appears different to each traveler upon it. For those whose closest music is sudden music, is this improvisation, or the following of a plan?

I don't know about your life, but mine is increasingly mediated by machines. Yet I have to forget these machines in order to venture forth in the world. Our tools need to be transparent but extending, if they are to improve us and get us to stretch ourselves. A good musical instrument does that, pulling us places that we can reach no other way. Although electronic media bring untold possibilities right into our homes, through the wires to the desktop and out through thrumming paper-cone speakers, the shakuhachi shows us that information really doesn't matter, focusing our attention instead in the single deep tone as it booms through resonating, welcoming space.

I wish I could focus on one single note—I am frazzled, spread too thin, doing too little though people say I do too much, staring out the window too many hours. Yet there is so much to see! Each day the mountain out my window changes to a darker, purpler color as the leaves on the trees embracing its slopes are wrenched away. Why are the evenings so much darker than I could ever imagine or remember before? This observation leads me to pay more attention. I am retreating from the city with its range, its ebb and flow, of influences. Each day I can play more notes on the flute. Why? I cannot say. Looking out the window I perhaps learn better how to inhabit the sound. Or perhaps not, perhaps I give myself too much credit. There is still nothing, no mastery, no tone, above all no discipline. I am stuck on the impossibility of this single tone, and I cannot escape it.

Shakuhachi music builds on the space surrounding each pure tone, with open, hollow melodies, deep precision, and tremendous emotion being articulated all at once. The Zen monks used blowing as a substitute for the chanting of sutras, intoning the words over and over again until specific meaning disappeared and the words rolled over into the churning syllables of emptiness, clearing the mind into a space of precision. The search for pure sound can do the same; it is neither exact nor emotional, but full of breath.

You can cushion your sound with oceans of air, or you can seek the most pure, the most exact result. That's what Giuffre wanted me to be after, a buoyed-up tone, floating over the fields of rhythm and chords. I never made him happy. Maybe I would today, but probably not. The only tone worth emulating is the one you can't quite reach, floating before you like a foghorn of destiny.

With time, the need for the familiar tune matters less. There is so much to concentrate on in the single sound. I envision a future where all I want is the truth, the infinite possibility, of a single tone. Only when this purity seems nearly within reach is one ready actually to play music, free of pretension or pride.

Or never mind music, think of the possibility of life with a solid core, not just the surface of infinite entertainments. We've all been there, surfing the channels of reality, buying some new toy to alleviate a lack of ease, choosing a new look. It's exciting but eventually exhausting, groundless, absent of purpose, of deep and meaningful grounding.

The history of the shakuhachi is fraught with mystery and obfuscation. Say its arrival in Japan was along the lines of the legend sketched above. It was one musical instrument among many, a folk flute, whose power of expression had not been seriously explored. Then for a time it became the tool of a sect half serious and half scam. You may have seen pictures of the *komuso* priests of the Fuke sect: ex-samurais wearing baskets over their heads, with only tiny slits to see through, wandering the countryside after the clan wars that had kept them in business for generations collapsed. In a pinch the fairly solid shakuhachi might make an effective club; most of the time, though, the roving mendicants were peaceful, playing mournful tones as they begged for alms (who could resist tossing a coin to the benefit of the pure sound?), sometimes spying for the authorities on the doings of the opposition.

It was all an act at first. Although the fabricated history of the Fuke sect traced the lineage of the flute to ancient Zen practices, the sect was strictly an innovation of the seventeenth century. But much of Zen mixes authenticity and chicanery in this manner. It's a game of logic, geared to twist your head to love emptiness instead of form; the Zen sound lures you not into music but into the absence of music.

Years later the Japanese government officially disbanded the Fuke sect because of its shady practices and tainted spirituality. In the mid-1800s the shakuhachi was "proclaimed" a musical instrument, not a spiritual tool. As if governments can decide such things! Despite these measures, however, the religiosity of the flute has only deepened with time.

Christopher Yohmei Blasdel, one of a handful of American shakuhachi masters, says:

The key word in learning and playing the shakuhachi is *listening*. One must listen with both the inner and outer ear. To listen with the outer ear means removing yourself to a place of relative quiet where you can hear and discern the myriad and wondrous sounds of nature and man's reaction to nature. . . . Listening with the inner ear means finding solitude within, away from the quotidian habits of thought, tensions, emotional highs and lows, and discerning the even more wondrous tones and melodies which constitute the human being at his deepest level.

Zen is not as strict as it appears on the surface. The message is simple: Get out of yourself, let the moment instruct you. But sometimes, to allow this, it is necessary to over prepare. Practice the same single tones for years. Admonish yourself for a lack of true discipline. Center the attention so that eventually, able to deny the focus, you will sit back and take it all in. It takes a long regimen of calm to allow wild flurries of energized action, to suddenly do something that matters, to sit down and find yourself suddenly alive, awake, at once inhabiting the tradition and ready at last to cast it all aside, leave the rules behind.

But with an instrument as difficult as this, there is no escape from the rules. They pull dreams back to reality—or else make them possible in the first place. Think of a spreading chaos of waxwings sailing erratically over a lake, cutting a curved swath through the wind. Though they are supposed to be migrating south, they swerve around to the north, the east, and dive toward the surface of the water, almost touching, then hurl themselves upward into the sky, looping, expanding, continuing their swirling trip toward a far destination that none of them could name, but all somehow know.

The wind making sounds, brushing life: the song that is everywhere. Blowing across a stalk of bamboo, you find a way to join in. The problem is not just learning to make a sound but figuring out how to *retain* that sound, that breath inside the whole, even in a modern life mediated by machines that few who use them comprehend. We still crave directness, even when we let electricity do all the singing—electricity, that word which before the wires meant something quite different. The energy needed to illuminate used to come from within: the body *electric*. Improvisation must build on memory.

The lips kiss the bamboo edge then back away. An air-pillowed sound arises, the choice comes: to go for clarity or for the cushion of breath. Change the pool of the flute to the peal of the bell. The empty bell in an empty sky, that old Zen picture. What do you hear, the metal, the air, the reverberation of waves? Or only the sound. Just this. Nothing to say about it, no way to replace. *Why then all these words?* Words exist not to make you read all as text but to allow you to take each phrase and be changed enough to turn away and listen anew. To place you close to the forces of air, push, breath, wood, growth, and earth, with little culture guarding the access. Everyone tries to follow the rules, but we all sound different. In losing the self you will find the self, by reducing (or expanding) effort into the single pure sound. When you get there, you could step into that shady thing called enlightenment, or be ready to return to music. It merely depends on your goal.

In 1823 Master Fuyo, a samurai and then a Zen blower of the Fuke sect, interviewed himself about trying to extract deeper meaning from the tones of the shakuhachi. Somehow his words sound as if they could have been written yesterday.

Please tell me, what makes a good player, and what makes a master?

A good player is one who makes the bamboo shaft *alive*. A master naturally and effortlessly brings forth something inconceivable. . . . You become the bamboo. The bamboo becomes you. A master lives in emptiness while working in form. . . .

Are there any masters living now?

There are none. I cannot even see a person who understands this practice.

Are you a master, a good player, or a poor player?

I am a master, I am a good player, and I am a poor player. I know the boundaries of mastery, but cannot enter. I do my practice in the realm of a good player, but have not reached the highest level. So doesn't that make me a very poor player? . . .

I cannot measure up to anyone. When I compare myself to my heart, I cannot measure up to my heart, and my heart does not measure up to me. . . . I just hold the bamboo and blow it.

Already people have stopped asking questions and have closed their mouths. What a waste of paper and ink to write this!

It is no surprise that he ends with the usual Zen admonishment: *What a waste! What a waste!* Fuyo seems to praise the asking of questions as much as he tries to give no answers. When I ask my teacher the reasons for certain practices and variations, he shakes his head: "That is just the way my teacher does it. I follow him." The questioning seems wrought out of the hierarchical system of mastery and apprenticeship. "And yet, and yet!" I naively believe this music to be full of individuality, that it is a place for free-wheeling experimentation to come to rest around a pure sound. *Your* pure sound. *My* pure sound. Each of us has our own exact tone between tool and idea. Instruction can only point toward it.

Patience, persistence: both are to be found in any story of real learning. In the last chapter I told a tale from my studies of the Tibetan wind instrument the gyaling. Before I headed for the mountain locale of Jumbesi to study with Lama Sangye Tenzin, I was in the Nepali capital of Katmandu, and one day I went at six in the morning to meet a monk who I was told might teach me. That first morning, he was too busy to see me. The next day I came back. "Still too busy," said his associate. The third morning: "Still busy today, so much to do here in the monastery." The fourth morning: "Ah, yes, today he has time to see you." And so the instruction began.

We did not speak a common language. He would play; I would try to repeat, usually with mistakes. He would smile and point a finger at his forehead, as if to say: "Listen, the mind, remember, keep it all inside." Every day, over and over again, the same few notes, the same struggle to put it all inside me.

Later I noticed that the teenage monks were all using tape recorders to record the music of the master! Then they would play along with the tape, rewind, play again. Technology helps even in the most ancient of spiritual practices. But it does not replace the pure instruments of feeling and of sound, which draw us out in a way the machine never will be able to. Still, there is no denying that technology is here to stay. If the old is to survive, it must live on *together* with the new.

Like performances of any classical music, shakuhachi recordings of the same piece are notoriously different from one another. When there are stringent rules to follow, performers must strive hard to make their individual contributions powerfully but subtly. It is no paradox that shakuhachi music is the most true to the rules even when it sounds utterly improvised. Sudden music can take hundreds of years to work its way into a tradition.

You may think its story obscure and far removed from our world, but in fact the shakuhachi is the root to a pure music that anyone can taste the power of. It is the voice of a Zen exactness that embraces ambiguity, the only kind of precision worthy of the wild wooliness of this world. Zen logic and literature are useful as we connect the patterns and rules we are taught the earth follows with the immediate implausibility of any actual moment: we don't know what is going to happen next, but we have laws and formulas and stories to help us along. Only with the possibility for endless improvisation does the world's heavy history leave room for us to move forward and change it.

To learn from any distant tradition, you have to look for inspiration within it and then make it your own. This belief led me to the *Blue Cliff Record,* one of the three major collections of original Chinese Zen koans. I did not explore it the way a true Zen student would, working closely with a teacher, banging my head against walls of empty logic in the long quest for sudden enlightenment. Rather, I was setting the words to music, taking the texts out of context, making a performance piece to be spoken along with sounds—a bit like Laurie Anderson, but perhaps with more gravity than levity. I was using these words because I liked them: their freshness, their exactness, their ambiguity.

I have since performed that piece all over the world, usually in out-of-the-way places, sometimes at academic gatherings where I was asked first to speak. "I will not speak," I would tell my inviters, "but I will perform," intoning these once sacred words lifted from their context, playing along on the clarinet, blending in with previously played sounds on a tape, trying to break through the wall another way, my own way. I do not know if it is the right way, but it is a way I have found myself traveling.

I like to think sacred texts exist to be pilfered, to be stolen and devoured, then spit out as something new. Zen in particular, however imbued it may be with respect for authority, demands a healthy contempt. "Is it true, Master, that all sounds are the voice of the Buddha?" "Yes, my child, it is true." "Well then, would the Master please stop sounding like a pile of shit?" Whereupon the Master struck the disciple soundly. Or take the case of the Master who comes across a bunch of monks arguing over a cat. He picks up the cat and demands that the monks speak up and end the dispute.

When no one dares speak, he cuts the poor cat in two. What a sense-less waste of feline life! This story may demonstrate the futility of arguments that go on and on. It certainly harks back to Solomon and two women's fight over a child. But the Zen monks are colder, their problems more abstract. They are willing to let an animal per-ish for their principles.

I always found that story too obvious, when simply told. The words needed to be tossed around, shuffled in and around each other like jokers in a deck of cards. It is up to us to decide if those monks were serious. And if so, about what? Are they abusing cats or pursuing enlightenment? The next koan solves the dilemma when a monk leans down, removes his sandals, and places them on his head. "Ah," the Master says, "you could have saved the cat."

Do whatever is least expected. Translate your life and its prin-ciples from a language you do not know. Throw the answers back and see if anyone catches them. I have always liked those cat stories but never been satisfied with them. Perhaps that is why I have never owned a cat. I would like them to own me, as in the stories. Perhaps I fear for their lives.

There's violence and defiance in these texts, and obvious as-saults on reason. But there are games to be played as well, logic problems with no solution, as in life itself. Our grasp of the texts will change with time, but at any moment we should be prepared to release what we know and test our understanding against the world. So we'll always be translating, and what we say will never be what we mean. Each time it will come out different, and we will pretend we understand what everyone else says, when what we re-ally want is to say it our own way.

The text, if it is truly as sacred as they say it is, must allow us this freedom. The words will become my own. Then I will offer them outward so they may be yours. When you meet them, change them.

Out of the hundred cases that make up the *Blue Cliff Record,* here are a few. Each presents the same clear tone—of ambiguity, of accidental success, of "Aha!"

CASE 75. NO REASON TO HIT

It's not easy, in words,
to tell shallow from deep,
and know who is guilty
and who needs to suffer.
Be more than example,
logic is no joke.

There is one way in and one way out,
as host or guest, you welcome the challenge.
To gather is easy,
to disperse is hard.
Wood calls for termites,
mirages encircle the sea.

It has been our purpose
to pull out pegs, and loosen nails,
to set thoughts free and untie what is bound.
This sets people loose where there's nothing to hold.
The ancient shore crumbles,
the ocean dries up. The mind is last to go.

One way, or many ways. How can a path encompass both answers at once? This is the essential question for any artist confronting a tradition, any student trying to get to the core of a practice. You want to be able to pack all into that single note, that single piece, that single stroke, and then repeat it over and over again—not the same note, but the same assiduousness, the same commitment, the same certainty that embraces uncertainty. Then you stun the world with all the activity that returns again to silence.

Blind, deaf, mute—no one can come near.
Soundless, without any play to the form
Can you make a choice?
What has that got to do with it!
laughing, crying
in dark and in light
Blind one! A true artist leaves no trace.
Deaf one! Let go of the point of words.
Mute one! Stick with the home of silence.

He could hear the ants fighting behind the mountain.
One chord on his lute and he knew we would lose.
The fall of the leaves, the bloom of the flowers,
Each marks the time under empty windows.

Can you speak? Or will you miss your chance again?

A sudden moment for a sudden sound, one chance for a sudden intervention. There is no need to speak, and there is nothing to do but speak. Each sound carries such portent, opens you up to such possibilities of hearing. Listen to the armies of ants; turn that into one beautiful sound. Hear the flowers open; mark the time with events. What is there to add to the constancy that the ever-changing world reveals? The improvised blurts out before you know just what to say.

No one has told us the one phrase before sound.
The single thread is still unbroken.

What is the body of wisdom?
An oyster gobbles the moon.
What is the purpose of wisdom?
A rabbit gets pregnant.

Without a moon, the pearls are few.
The moon comes out, rabbits swallow the light.

This mindmoon alone and full—

People these days just stare,
drive spikes into empty space.
One sliver of empty air,
ties your self to the place.

Silent and speaking, language before words. The single tone of the reverberant bamboo flute answers these questions as it listens to the wind. These images from the Zen tradition offer images to the music, but explain nothing except the need to keep practicing, whatever it is you practice, and to continue learning to listen to the world.

Stand in the shadow of the masters as they walk: but shadows move and one can never catch them. Shakuhachi music endures as a practice between religion and art precisely because of its mixture of the planned and the sudden, the notated and the improvised. Unlike Tibetan music, which sounds planned but in fact is never put down on paper, shakuhachi music, though it often sounds extemporaneous, is written down with great precision. Its notation uses a unique alphabet of tones and diacritical marks for both rhythm and inflection. When does interpretation break from the plan and become impromptu? Right from the outset there are so many ways to play just that one note. To deviate from the notation is against the rules. The notation was fixed for fear that the shakuhachi tradition would fall into confusion. If you play only according to your feelings, even if the sound of the bamboo is heard as beautiful, you will not realize the Zen quality of shakuhachi. But if, in blowing, you experience the emptiness of shakuhachi, then there is no need to be concerned with notation.

"You are a person and I am a person . . . , yet there are great differences," continues Master Fuyo. In music, the single tone is only a place to begin, it is never meant to be enough. Indeed, the single tone is impossible to achieve. The flute will never emulate the empty bell in an empty sky. We will never comprehend the sound; we will never produce the sound. We will listen as it fades away over the looming mountainside, evading us like the sinking whistle of a passing train. It is the sound at the end of the rainbow, just out of reach, beyond the range of the ear and human ability.

The instrument should suddenly take you to sounds you never thought you could create. Then you listen as you play back and realize there is no thought before the action; no melody before the breath, before the actual happening; no ideas but the sounds. You cannot prepare for this sudden insight, as much as you practice, as much as you test your abilities left and right and blow on and on into exhaustion.

When you one day know how to play it, the shakuhachi might not be so different from any other instrument. The method becomes you, you become the method. Any instrument, any practice worth learning, is something we can get inside and then forget that we know. There is no boundary between the player and the played. The shakuhachi just makes this basic link visible, because that is what it offers. Shakuhachi. Clarinet. The play of Zen phrases and inadvertent words. Pick an instrument, start to learn it. Then wonder how much of its history you need to know to really get it.

I offer no moral guidance on how to turn this musical way into life, as opposed to art. All I can say is, if you learn how to put the greatest of attention into a simple act, all this practice will pay off. Never forget that this art is not for yourself alone, but for the world. The pure tones are to be played outward, toward a place in nature, toward a community that wants to listen.

The time will come when you must depart from the path and enter the dark woods, seeing neither forest nor trees but only uncertainty, the deep unknown. Although the tool itself explains nothing, you *will* need music to survive. All these tones slip out of the environment, rising up as figure from the ever-present ground. Out the window there's an analogy: the mountain has no real edge today; the lines of the ridge and summit are confused by clouds. It's like a charcoal sketch, not a solid ridge. There are always the changing trees up there: sometimes they have leaves, other times their crisped twigs are rimed in ice. The ridge disappears with a wind gust of white fog; the mountain moves. It never appears to the eye suddenly, obviously there. No, it wafts up from the valleys and can be seen many ways.

The real notes blur, the earth's notes, the music that prefigures human nature. The shakuhachi wants us to grasp that. Although I do not practice incessantly, every time I pick up my flute it seems I discover something new, I am lured in more deeply. The tool incites the practice; we carry around the baggage of music tied up, bound in a sack.

The poetic Zen master Ikkyu (1394–1481), also known as "Crazy Cloud," wrote several poems in praise of the shakuhachi. Starting with his sentiments, I've rewritten them into my own travels, my own fears:

Shakuhachi blown alone plays sorrow too hard
to take, it's a flute from a faraway land, calling
from the edge of the country.

Played right in Times Square,
whose song is it then?

This is why Zen people have no friends.

*

The master now roams the heavens as well as the earth.
Still, his shakuhachi pulls you to invisible worlds.
So forget the universe, pull back, sit still:

this song is enough
one flute player here

world in a long breath
earth in bamboo
forget the tune, one tone
is enough, the sound

of inevitable air.

Seasons change, the song is torn
that old flute splits straight from the lip to the bone.

My flute itself is fragile and, like all shakuhachis, it will one day split apart. Play it continuously until it can take no more. Living bamboo cannot be frozen. Compressing all music into one outburst, I try still to contain my cry: Why work for years only to be satisfied with just one note? Why fear commitment to self-imposed exile, where you will seem unworthy to play even the simplest song? One note begins the journey, and one note will end it.

"It takes horseshit," Ikkyu also said, "to grow bamboo. But it too longs forever, weeps, begs to the wind." I'm longing, too, for that perfect sound, for that one-note history, the pale single tone that contains all other tones ever heard before or that will someday be heard. That one most resonant of all tones, which contains all octaves and harmonics in one unplaceable sound. Inside that single note I want too much: endless, unstoppable, sudden inspiration, like a wall of organ pipes surrounding me and growing from an infinitesimal whistling to immense rumbling, then cutting all away to be satisfied with just one tone.

By confusing the familiar, changing the meanings of the words and senses you know, the truth is approached like a spider and its prey stuck in a web: one dances nimbly over it, the other is fatally trapped. Which side better expresses the fate of a single tone? The one note must contain more than it can possibly contain. The cloud on the horizon must be bigger than any possible mountain, and the song stays inside you even after you're all played out. Hold on to it forever and you will always be ready to begin.

ROADS, MUSIC, RAPTURE

Why work so hard at the single tone, struggling for years to achieve something that no one else will hear as well as you? The answer is easy: total pleasure, total dissolve, envelopment in the landscape beyond, the possibility of ultimate rapture in mellifluous sound. Is the most ecstatic music the most needed music? Why not play, get lost, disregard logic or the need to explain the pleasure that comes when we get carried away?

Yet allow a question to arise, which will no doubt lead to another, and soon you will feel lost again, perplexed, smothered by doubt. That's the moment to start singing, I tell you, to let out a piercing wail as the late Nusrat Fateh Ali Khan so often did, pushing your hands against the air as if to clear the sky for the ultimate lament, the total song where joy and sadness are conflated into one supreme emotion. Or as the jazz pioneer Buddy Bolden, gone crazy on a single note held forever ninety years ago in New Orleans, did. For the best music is neither giddy nor portentous, major nor minor, pathetic nor glib. It inhabits pure uncertainty and forces oneness out of the opposites that attract this world into being, out of empty, deflecting forces.

In music I tend to forget my self. I am subsumed in the far, inexact power that sound is able to express about human movement and audible escape. I'm lost in it; for a while, nothing else matters. It becomes a beauty I make, a work inseparable from me, the player, the improviser. Complete absorption in it rarely happens—when it does, it doesn't last long—but I remember it for years.

That ecstasy inside the art of sound is not so much pure pleasure as escape from individual meandering into an essential oneness with the unspeakable meaning of the world. No one will ever be able to tell you what is, or why, in words. The celebration in sound seems like a language, but it is not a language. Why not? Because you can love it and share in it even if you have no idea what is being said.

Gently spinning dervishes lifting their feet softly above the ground; a circle of quivering Balinese monkey chanters shaking their hands forward and inward in a pulsing circle; Hasidic *nigunim,* sacred melodies that never resolve: spiritual musics such as these are known for their ecstasy, but rapturous emotion can also be found in any music that gathers our usually diffuse energy together and draws it toward a single point. That point then erupts in the shout or the song, the concentrated melody, an intensity that seems not merely pleasant but *necessary,* a sound so present it is impossible to refute.

Sometimes there are elaborate reasons for the existence of such music, stories that explain why it can possibly matter so much. Take this parabolic tale by the eighteenth-century Reb Nachman, explaining how the world is:

> At one end of the world there is a mountain; on the top of the mountain, there is a fountain. And the water springs forth without ceasing. At the other end of the world lies the heart of the world, and although all things have a heart, the heart of the world is more worthy than any human heart. So at one end of the world is the fountain that gushes from the summit crags, and at the other end is the heart of the earth.
>
> Now, the heart is stuck at one end, the fountain way at the other. But the heart is in love with the mountain spring, it is filled with an unutterable, endless longing for that distant geyser of water spraying straight from the faraway peak. The heart cannot move; it lies scorched by the sun, but it stares at the mountain so far away, and, barely visible, it sees the gushing water. Since the waters roar only at the summit, they can always be seen, even from thousands of miles away. If the heart were to lose sight of the spring for even one instant, it would cease to live. If the heart would die, then all the world would die, for the life of the world is contained within the life of its heart.
>
> Once the heart tried to get closer to the fountain, but when it moved just a bit closer the water fell out of view, so it could not proceed, as it needs to be able to see the water to remain alive.
>
> So what happens, you ask, when night falls over the world? The heart becomes dark with grief, for as the sun falls the water stops glistening in the distant sun, and the earth's heart will die of longing, and when the heart is dead all the earth and all creatures on this earth will die.
>
> As the day draws to a close, the heart begins to sing farewell to the mountain waters, singing its grief in a wild, astonishing melody, while

the mountain spring sings farewell to the heart. Their songs are filled with endless love and longing.

So why does it continue? Why isn't the world long dead and gone if even one night brings with it such impossible sadness? That's why we are here. The true and attentive human being keeps watch over the situation. In that last moment before the day is done, and the spring is gone, and the heart dead, and the world over, a good person comes and gives a new day to the heart, and the heart gives the new day to the spring, and so they live again.

When the day returns, it too returns with melody, and with strange and beautiful words that contain all wisdom. And there are differences between each day and every other. And each day comes with its own song, a song that no one has ever seen or heard before. And as long as there are good people, true musicians, on this earth, this new day will not be the last.

You don't have to sing the sun up like Orpheus as much as wake up to a sense of longing, to want something far away that you can never reach. You're not supposed to reach it. What matters is to want it. Every note must exude desire. There is a tragedy in this, because as soon as you've created such a note, it is gone. Music is the art that leaves as soon as it arrives; it always comes to us *suddenly,* and departs the same way. It stays with us only if its power is so pure and so strong that it binds artist and audience with a message deeper than can be conveyed by any spoken language. Whatever it may *do* to us, there is a sense in which music speaks nothing beyond itself, standing for no emotion, no story outside its ways of rhythm and timbre. It cannot be doubted, it cannot be explained. Its passion can only be talked around, never represented or recounted.

And yet it concerns itself with everything as much as with nothing. You don't need to understand it to know it or to love it. When it works it speaks to people of many worlds. The best of all musics have this emphatic and essential side. The music must seem necessary, impossible not to play or to hear. It answers to no one yet calls out to all. Seeking it out brings comfort as much as adventure.

Read a story, learn it, then forget the words. Now, play it in sound. If you don't like that story, pick another. Internalize it; hold on to the feeling it produces in you. Strip away the plot, hold on only to the feeling. Use that to lure from within you spontaneous music.

Love is about the search, the longing, the striving for the pure sound you'll never quite reach. Ecstasy is something else: the deep pleasure that actually arrives, that is there for the taking. I find that it is impossible to doubt music while playing it. Even as the rest of my life seems overpopulated with questions, with uncertainties about why one thing should be done instead of another, in the midst of the playing, the dancing around silence and space in the presence of notes, music always seems to matter.

Mattering is in itself not enough, though. I still want to reach for those notes that *must* be played, that are right because they are essential melodies, unavoidable tones, songs that cannot be defied. This music is silent even when it sings because it does not speak, it cannot be reduced by explanation. Musical mystics are often smiling, laughing, crying with joy as they sing songs that spread the human spirit not above the world but out into it, mingling with colors, species, winds. You must make these notes matter almost too much, such that you can't imagine the sound ever stopping and an instant holds an eternity of pleasure.

The best art is both certain and ambiguous at once. You don't know why it matters so, you don't know what it's for. It falls between cracks of genre and purpose, neither popular nor ascetic, earthy nor mannered, raw nor refined, but in between all categories and rules, transcending any categories critics wish to apply to it. You need not know anything about it to love it; feeling it grab hold of you, you will not want to turn it off or down, yet neither will you feel it is manipulating you or stealing your soul.

For perfection may be a dream, but ecstasy is never beyond our reach. It's right there in the accessible realm of rough delight. Who are the true musicians when sound is now everywhere, in the soundtrack of our lives, seeping out of invisible speakers impossible to turn down? All I have is a few stories that point in the direction I mean. I've trapped them on the move. You only find these moments away from home. That's why travels continue to lead to an improvised kind of destiny. Pack your bags . . .

After a year living in Norway, a land that takes care of its own, I'd had it with lack of danger. It was virtually impossible to get into trouble there. But then I heard about a part of town that was scheduled for demolition, or at least gentrification, where the few who really wanted to resist the system that took care of all of your needs hung out, at a club called Den norsk guruformidling A/S, or "The Norwegian Guru Exchange, Inc." This rebel café stayed open all night, with music and drink available to all, pay what you would, what you could.

On walking through the rusted door, I spied an old clarinet tacked up on the wall, purely for decoration. Taking it down, I found the reed was still good. I unscrewed the ligature, moistened the cane, and set it carefully back on the cool crystal-glass mouthpiece. The instrument was still in order; music would be possible. In the next room a bearded character was waving a huge sword around. Suddenly he screamed and plunged it into a wooden table, then he calmed down. The table had a lot of sword marks; this Viking probably did that quite often. "Don't worry," someone reassured me. "Jens is a complicated person, but he isn't dangerous."

A woman with long stringy red hair had picked up a guitar and was strumming completely unfamiliar chords, something like a mixture of the blues, ancient folk music, and Jimi Hendrix detuning his guitar. *This* sounded like something new. Everyone was listening, dancing in the corner or gradually getting ready to join in. She started to sing, and her voice cried another kind of blues, not the down-home bending notes that went back to the griots of West Africa, but something out of the arctic tundra, a wail like wind racing through the trees. This sound could be on no record, could not be taken down. The room was listening closely, everyone huddled together, resisting the system that seemed impossible to resist.

That was the most beautiful voice I've ever heard, and I know I'll never hear anyone sing like that again—and if that's not true I'll make it true because the experience will increase and grow and replicate itself as I repeat it inside, and wait years to write it down, and change enough details so that it will fade in precision enough for all of you to ask the question, "What is the most beautiful voice you've ever heard?" and you'll fill in the blank with your own memory. But here the voice was more than just a voice because the whole place was reverberating with the need for that voice, and everyone needed each other and needed music so much that nothing else seemed to matter. It wasn't blared out in an amplified thunder, but quiet, impossible to hear without concentration, which made it deeper, more beautiful, more strange, so much more than anything you could ever repeat or in any way capture.

Writing about music can never substitute for it. The story necessarily surrounds an amazement that is largely private. As in Frank Conroy's meticulous novel *Body and Soul*, where a young composer discovers jazz and how to integrate it with the classical tradition. He's in an automat on 42nd Street and he meets some jazz musicians, who can tell he's a musician too. One old guy writes some chord symbols on a napkin, and the kid is amazed, he sees, he grasps the significance of those sketchy marks and realizes there's a whole new world out there of changing tonality that he must somehow get ahold of. But just then the old guy collapses into his milkshake, dead, ODed on drugs. The kid understands that there's something deadly and destructive about the world he has just gained access to. In the end, it turns out, he was not meant to grasp it, and in time he will turn away. In that sense, he ends a failure. And there's nothing he could have done about it. The romance of the impossible sound: *you can't describe it, you never even heard it.*

They say the streets of New Orleans are paved with music. This is the birthplace of jazz, voodoo, and Cajun cuisine, all in one. Music streams out of every door on Bourbon Street, and hecklers lure the visitor in to debauchery. A grinning demonic face flashes: "Live Orgy" on the front, and on the back, "It's Wild." You want to peer in the door to see what's going on, but it all seems like a trap. The town is far more troubling than I imagined, a caricature of the society of music, a French Quarter—Quartier Latin—devoted to the almighty dollar of the tourist. Yes, that's right, I'm trying to discredit the place so I won't have any fun. It's obvious I haven't paid the three bucks to sit on the benches in Preservation Hall and hear the old-timers conjure up Buddy Bolden's ghost as they have for eighty years. Some of these guys are almost a hundred years old. They may have *played* with Buddy, heard him play that one last note that stopped him cold.

I didn't think I could find any surprises here, in a place that had become a caricature of itself. I didn't know whether to be taken in by the glitter and hazy decay or run away, down a side street. It was hot as hell.

I remembered a small café my local anarchist friend Max Cafard proudly said was "still cool, a haven for rebels in this city of revels." I turned off the main drag and ventured on until I came to the place. It was a little run down, had a few too many mirrors on the walls; the creaky ceiling fans spun slowly, unevenly, around and around. Mere seconds after I'd sat down, a wizened old fellow with a slight tremor, looking like a prospector just in from the gold rush, leaned toward my table and, looking me straight in the eye, said in a firm voice: "Excuse me. You don't look like you're from around here. I would guess you're from Europe. Am I right?"

Wondering how my face might reveal all those strange years in Iceland and Norway, I responded: "Not exactly."

"Well then," he tried again, "you must be a musician."

"Right this time. You?"

"Well, I lived for years roaming around Eastern Europe, you know, before the wall came down, playing on all the old church organs I could find. They have this incredible *sound,* just to touch them, make it come out."

"What kind of music were you playing? Jazz?" I asked, knowing I was in New Orleans, talking with an old-timer.

"Not exactly jazz. But improvised. From the soul. The name's Crawford. Harold Crawford. You know, back in the fifties, in New York, I was hanging out in the Cedar Bar with the expressionists. Jackson Pollock, I was his friend. They were the ones who understood the music. The artists could see what I heard, what I was playing. They were the people I connected with.

"Back then in Eastern Europe, you know, before the changes, the artist was respected. Music was respected. People could help me do what I wanted to do. But then it all fell apart."

True. This old guy, nose red from too much drink or sun or something, was making sense. Before the end of the cold war, the famous Bulgarian State Radio and Television Female Vocal Choir had been the Communist ideal of national culture. Now they've got drum machines and managers in Manhattan.

Harold was in the West, though, too. "Yes, and then there was October 11, 1988, in Vienna. The grand cathedral, in the center of town. That was a fantastic event. Indescribable music. I was play-ing that organ. In the center of Vienna."

Ecstatic music is always indescribable. That's why it survives, binds people together, cannot be talked about or told in words. October 11, 1988. Vienna. Wait a minute! I think as I walk down the street after leaving the café. I was there, staying in a pensione on the Graben after having traveled by barge from Bulgaria for a week. I walked past the cathedral and heard the strange, out-of-place quality of the music. I almost went in, but decided to walk on. And now this?

I wanted to run back and tell Harold this. Why? To say I was in Vienna and had *almost* gone to his concert, only to meet him seven years later in New Orleans, a place that follows its own beat. No, better move on. I doubt I will see Harold Crawford again. But mu-sic brings meaning to the chance encounter, as we inhale sounds that we can only imagine, since they were never heard.

Arriving once in Montreal, I called a friend of mine, Margie Gillis, a rather well known solo dancer who travels the world giving recitals. It turned out she was performing at the Place des Arts that evening; in fact, she was doing one dance to a piece of my music, which I had given her in 1986 and never seen performed. She got me a ticket to the sold-out performance, where I joined about a thousand other people in the audience.

The music was an improvisation based on a lament by Bartók that I had recorded in 1986 with cellist Eugene Friesen in the cav-ernous Cathedral of St. John the Divine in New York. It is a slow, mournful call that repeats three times, each time going unan-swered. Margie turned it into a dance duet (which she performed with her brother) about a clinging boy who refuses to let his girl go, when all she wants is be free.

Listening to that old, slightly out-of-tune recording, clearly played on my number-two clarinet while the good one was in the shop, I remembered that when I recorded the piece I was totally distraught over my girlfriend's decision to leave me and escape to Nepal. I had just flown home from Cornwall to see her, and she'd simply said, "Good-bye, I'm off to Katmandu." All I could do was go into the huge, echoing cathedral and cry on the clarinet. Now here, six years later, I was watching as my own story was danced in front of me.

What did it mean? Does this kind of thing bring people closer together? Everyone wants to pursue his or her own path. Someone is crying in the cottonwoods of Sedona, and a part-time composer sits in a huge auditorium as a thousand people listen to his music, nobody aware that he is there. I liked that. Complete anonymity while the record of my drawn-out emotion rumbled over and over from the past on into the future, with me back as a mute witness to a pain mixed with joy and awe.

The record of musics heard and unheard, of links between places and people real or imagined, is an unending din of convulsing memories. From here it goes on late into the night, to other cities, to other ecstatic tensions and releases, on to the forced international immediacy of New York. I think of the time I lived above the Ear Inn, a Manhattan hangout nearly on the Hudson River, way downtown. There, on Monday nights, the legendary clarinet master Perry Robinson and his band would start playing at midnight. Always one of my heroes, he would shout out "Maestro!" when I entered the club, and he sometimes let me join in.

The man on the squeeze-box leans into the microphone and starts crooning the tale of Buddy Bolden, a story that I keep hearing over and over again, inside my recollections and all over the world. What happened to him? What was he thinking about all those years? What did that one note do to him? He needed to play it, he needed to get lost, there was no other way.

Perry calls me up to the stage: "Now do it, your turn, *play like Buddy, like this is the last note you will ever let loose.*" Then I knew just where the history of jazz began and where it went wrong, how that first note released the madness of our century's sudden music conjured up on the spot, and I'm up there, it's two A.M., and I'm privileged to stand by the master as he leads me into a Russian folk tune, "Moscow Nights," that he first recorded in the sixties. The impossible memories are the ultimate refrain, the sound and the stories, the memory and the moment, the master and the student. All sounds are Buddha's voice, all one, all none. We cry out for something we can barely see, a goal that we will never attain although it is always right here. For an instant, I question no more. Far from this city lie the fountain and the heart, the mountain and the desert of the world. I taste the wet song with my dry, parched tongue.

I can feel the elusive ecstasy slip away. I keep wanting the feeling and am unable to sit still. It's time to move on, to seek the comfort of the road. The adventures I have are sporadic gasps amid innumerable aimless wanderings. After all those years stuck on the search for the one true note, I find it is when I'm on the move, away from the practice, that the songs finally emerge. The music is fomented at home but designed for the world. It must always be a surprise, always new, always sung somewhere else. Could it be the same song every time? Never. That would not be improvisation. The subtlest differences are the greatest and most necessary changes. The greatest pleasures are achievable, but they are momentary, fleeting, and I hope it is not true that they are only achievable far from home, suddenly, on the traveler's trail, on a musical journey, not at a fixed musical place.

Must we always be moving to find these ultimates? Or does one need a home to get the most out of travel, artistic or eventful travel, motion inside or out? It is a rapture in motion that one finds on the road.

What is this road that multiplies singularity, keeps one from going crazy over a single note so deep and so long? Is there really a path from the world's heart to that high-up fountain?

The road. It's the way from here to there. The musician's middle name. The open sky and the lines traveling. It's how places get meaning moving.

On the parkway for months now, there's been a special sign that I see every time I drive by: three solid neon-green digital lines, horizontal. It's meant as some kind of warning, but there's never anything wrong. Instead it is an I Ching trigram offered to the streaming commuters, three solid lines, the power of Heaven: *pure aggression*. Complete yang, full steam ahead; no receptivity to balance the forward movement.

We wish the ride could always be so smooth, but the road also goes back the way we came. The paved snake across the desert, the proof that people can traverse any land, even if it doesn't want us. There's at least a path just about everywhere, even through those "roadless areas" on the maps; people push places around with machines that don't say no.

I remember an Eskimo, an old man when he came down from the ice, the child of Robert Peary and an Inuit woman. When asked what most impressed him about our warm southern lands, he said: the roads. "Perhaps," he mused, "they have been here since the beginning of time." Indeed, we act as if they have always been here, taking for granted the possibility to move along them, to speed to-ward the horizon from one mirage to the next.

Road noise: the car hits a rock, the tire splatters, there is a whirr, a twist, we roll into the mud on the side of the road . . . all of a sud-den I am alone . . . the mist sinks over an empty wilderness. There is no way to get anywhere! All modern errands are impossible in this forest off the asphalt line. Lucky for me I don't want to be any-where but here; I'd rather sit and let the car melt like the snow does at the edge of the road.

The road is only the beginning of this story, though. When I de-cide to hold on to an image, it can be with me for years. You can choose to stake a home down in a village, by a wall, or in a grove of trees, but if you're in this world you probably know where you live by its place on the road, a number on a named street, a code that makes you easy to find. A place on the road—that's right: you can get there from here.

Road joy, not rage. I am talking about the pleasure of move-ment, of finding new sounds and new worlds. I used to think, com-ing across a new village or a new angle or a new vista, "Here, yes, here would be a fine place to stop and to stay forever." Why not? All it would take would be a reason, or an emotion, or a sudden beauty or pleasure. The single tone soars off into arpeggios and slides and wild shrieks and calls that reverberate endlessly off the edge of the cliff of incompleteness or doubt.

The communication of the ecstatic, total pleasure is not the same as being consumed by the pleasure. The sudden release is at once so much and so little, a bewildered wondering after so much search and effort: "That's it? That's all there is?" And then it's time at once to start again, with the yearning again seeming more than the release.

If you are the music while the music lasts, what happens once it's done? The best pop songs grow on you as you play them over and over again, as they seem to take over the times. Soon they are forgotten, then a few years down the line they reemerge as a kind of nostalgia.

Improvised music is not supposed to ever return, for it will never be played the same way again, but because of recordings improvised solos are immortalized as well. Frozen music is constructed bit by bit out of sudden cries for joy, and this too is listened to again and again. Who can tell if a record was improvised or written down? Maybe there's little difference, because in each performance what matters is that the musicians are making notes come alive and sing.

If you sense the spontaneous excitement of all the players together, then you're close to the sudden joy. Music may well be the ecstasy that lasts as it flows, the exuberance that goes on. And on. As the melodies are rising and swirling, think of the smiles deep inside. Extend that moment's pleasure, a pleasure that is so close to pain. Envelop the extremes with the tones that can keep rising, on and on.

In Arabic music, it is thought that the performer must be in a state of sustained ecstasy to make the crowd swoon. "The moon," says singer Sabah Fakhri, "only reflects the light it receives from the sun." Audience and musician stand thus in rapt attention with each other, carried away into that land of pure music that leaves all else behind. Like those Turkish dervishes spinning gently toward God, slowly feeling their feet lift off the ground as they pull themselves, if not to Heaven, then toward that high, spirited place: ecstasy remains with you. There is no longing once enlightenment has pulled you up to its home. You're there, and there you stay.

When asked just what they mean by holding themselves and their audience in a vibrant, ecstatic embrace, some Arab musicians have refined the idea, speaking of "modal ecstasy" or *saltanah,* meaning "reigning over; to feel mastery, to be in control or in

charge." In Middle Eastern music there is plenty of improvisation, rarely over chord changes but rather within modes of possibilities; within any one scale, for example, the musician must
use different pitches going up than going down, and there may
in addition be special kinds of ornamentations or acts the player
must perform at particular places along the rise and fall. You're
in saltanah when you're so far gone into the mode that you can't
imagine anything else to life, any other modes, any other songs,
any other way to be than tumbling and twisting inside the roil of
the music, where you have dissolved yourself or enhanced your self
by *becoming* the sonic rules themselves, thereby showing just how
much hope and difference can be found in these pure and beloved
constraints.

It's a continuous state but a fragile state, easy to be disrupted by
even the slightest change in position or attunement or attention.
You must work to hold it there. Still, it is not meant to end. Maybe
it's not a destination; maybe it's still the sustenance of the longing,
of the grasping for a perfection that you'll never be able to find.
There's only so much that music can be. However you enter its
charms—as a player, as a listener by choice or imposition, as a
writer trying to put its ephemerality into words—you will not succeed in freezing it. It disappears as soon as it has come.

Moments bind information together into poetry—though you
might need to go out and climb a mountain or run ten miles before you feel it. Those moments, too, come and go, but what you
can discover in them remains. Out of the madness comes meaning.
There's no need to completely lose yourself when so much can be
suddenly discovered.

Musically, you face the consequences of one moment's decision
by being forced to go somewhere else, up or down the scale, delv-

ing deep into the mode or enjoying a break from the rules. The sudden music is the ecstatic moment because of how it works, because it won't be found ever exactly again. The spontaneous life does the same, finding joy instant by instant, yet not detaching one from responsibility. It all has to fit together. At the same time, it all makes me want to keep moving, to propel myself with accident through many places: my path is the improvisation that answers the question of how all my facets are meant to be one, that responds when a sudden muse intervenes to tell you to go left, not right, to nudge you toward a series of discoveries that are empty until you sing a melody that binds them.

So the improviser must wander, always ready to create anew, in a different place, a different time. Once is never enough for the perfect moment. You will want more of them. The next one will be completely different.

When I strive to remember such perfect moments I discover a block inside you. The past is hazy, fading. My home doesn't resemble its appearance on the unintelligible foreign news. The city I find myself in is beautiful as the sun sets over water, and the alabaster buildings red and golden but mute. I do not fit in. I have been moving long enough to be unsure how to go home or what people will want from me there. Will I be seen as a foreigner at home as well? Or as a jaded wanderer, full of nothing but anecdotes. Where, after all these journeys, is my core? Have I forgotten the quest, from heart to mountain, along a once gushing but now trickling stream?

Home, invisible. Practices, forgotten. Indifference. Doubt.

Exile? It's easy to take yourself too seriously and exaggerate the meaning of a situation, of a loneliness that makes you want to create but keeps you from fitting in. The song ought to have a light quality, despite this inner doubt. It should reflect the lost musings

of a traveler walking rhythmically out to the plaza at the edge of a
powerful, cold sea:

> The signs they make no sense.
> The subtitles are immense
> Too many languages in your head at once,
> they're asking too much from you here in exile.
>
> On the esplanade where ships come in
> people walk along in pairs
> and you will never join them
> through their absent morning stares
> as the sky turns gold to red
> the earth leaves you to be led
> and you follow in her footsteps now in exile.
>
> In exile
> from the home you never had
> in exile
> from those who said that you were bad
> from the ones who know you best
> who put you through those futile tests
> to assess your suitability for exile.
>
>> My country doesn't want me
>> they've forgotten I exist
>> I crossed the easy border
>> It was not difficult to resist
>>
>> But I wouldn't play their game
>> the confession was not signed
>> I couldn't turn my friends in
>> I wouldn't toe the line
>
> Now many years have gone by
> Time has taken me for a ride
> They have forgiven everything,

They want me on their side.
The empty house awaits me,
I could pack my bags today
You wonder why I stay?
Because I only get ideas when I'm in exile.

If I go home I'm doomed
to repeat myself and then
You will tire of me easily,
and send me off again.
I will have to find a cause
I will have to listen for love
and learn to read those endless words
the crazy scripts, the flashing lights
the slippery streets, rain turns to ice
the early frost, and never lost
the rhythm's clear, to have no fear
so far off, walking, happy, home, in exile.

On the road you'll feel me reach you
from some sad cyberian café
Inside, you'll try to touch me
but I'm nowhere long to stay
When I check I'm only blinking
on your electric screen, just
beaming in my messages from exile.

  You know these words
  will be for no one, no one else but you.
  I know that you can take them
  although you never wanted to,

  I'll try my best to go so far
  that I'll really find something new,
  'cause when I meet you next
  you might be ready then for exile.

It is the same yearning, the same hope, the same gleam, that keeps us moving for years on end. We still want the surprise, the joy, the movement, the journey to those places where we improvise upon what we find. That's the art worth doing on the run.

Do not settle for an easy homelessness. Stick to those places that will remember you after you've gone. Go home only when it wants you back. Something is stalking you: an echo, a shadow; what the music leaves when it's gone.

THE SHADOW IS WHAT YOU HEAR

What kind of space does music leave when it suddenly stops? Why can't you get that song out of your head? No music lasts forever, but it is our memories of sound that make us beg for more. How can we keep it around longer; how do we notice what surrounds it, what keeps it in? There are clues in the idea of the shadow, and how it carries across the senses into the realm of sound. Music once gone leaves shadows of its sound, in echoes, in memory, in the silence that remains when the tones are no more.

Shadows do not reveal the true shapes of things. In their transparency they lie. A pole bends up the side of a building. A child becomes twenty feet long on the sidewalk. The nearness of the mountain makes the village beneath it dark all day. Though we can't feel it, the shadows tell us of the sun. They tell where the light comes from, and the proximity and position of the bright things gleaming in the world. In the shadows, separate objects blur. Shadows always remind us of the opposite of day.

Why should there ever be separate things? Could we see a world where we float through objects, or where we are stopped by the black solidity of a shadow? Things hold their separate meaning only for a while, then fade into dusk. You have to hide in the shadows because there's no other way to be free.

Shadows are not only seen, but fall in the wake of the other senses as well. Tasting shadows? When you eat breakfast in a dream and awake to find you're still hungry. Smelling shadows? Easy. Any wafting smell is a shadow. Scents detached from the other senses are hints of happenings and associations. Touching shadows? The feel of an aura, a body that isn't quite there. Hearing shadows? *What in the world is that noise?* The echo of a sound that was or never was quite there.

And what of the shadows that blur between the boundaries of sense? The heavy noise of crushed snow under boot. The weight of conscience, the force of the line on the beach left by the tide. When you come to sense everything as a mere trace of something harder, lighter, more solid, and more real, that's when the shadow comes to know you, not you the shadow. Beyond the crisp late daylight lies a blur, an illusion that means we will never be able to grasp what holds this world together, a void that cannot even be thought about. When you finally catch up with the shadow, it will certainly tell the truth.

You can loom over it and trick it into shrinking away, into disappearing into the dark, but it will not stay still once you begin to move. The shadow proves that your body will still stop light. That's normal, and it is why beings that do not cast a shadow are suspect —questionable at best, and evil at worst. Seeing the shadow this way is obvious; letting it take you as the sun disappears behind the mountain in the afternoon may cast a weight on the soul, but it is nothing to worry about. There is no time to run to the other side of the mountain, no way to escape the setting of the sun except to turn on a light. This easy option is as false as a painting of sunrise plastered over a west-facing window. All you need to do to see the shadow is to turn away from the sun. All you need to forget it is to close your eyes.

A musical shadow could be illusion, or it could be the lingering memory of a sound that makes it matter all the more. If you manage to block out all sound, you will have no trouble discerning the basic warp and woof of the world, but you will feel like an outsider, detached from the goings-on. Maybe your mind will be singing the song of the Tibetan gyaling that I learned many years ago. Sound puts us into the picture, or makes the picture more than a mere image. Up in arctic lands, the Inuit asks the visitor coming in out of the cold to "speak, so that I may see you." Do the same: add a voice, even a whisper, and in so doing, make the other really there.

Around us everywhere are sounds, easy to miss, just like the ornaments on the roofs and facades of buildings that we miss out on if we keep our eyes glued to the sidewalk. There is so much to listen to that we must ignore it just to live, instead concentrating on whatever task we have set out to do. But if you choose to listen, really listen, you might hear that you in fact belong. Consider what Edmund Carpenter learned from living many years with the Inuit in northern Canada, that territory recently renamed and returned to its people as Nunavut: "Auditory space has no favored focus. It's a sphere without fixed boundaries, space made by the thing itself, not space containing the thing. It is not pictorial space, boxed in, but dynamic, always in flux, creating its own dimensions moment by moment. . . . The eye focuses, pinpoints, abstracts. . . . The ear, however, favors sound from any direction."

So where are the shadows in this world of sound that surrounds us? Explore the various meanings the word *shadow* can have in the afterglow of sound. An express train barrels through the station without stopping, its sharp whistle rising then falling in pitch as it slides away. The Doppler effect. Then faintly you hear a whistle from the opposite mountain, a call from the other side of the river. The first echo. And then there's another, from the mountain above. The sound bounces back and forth, seeming now to be in constant motion—not an object, but a play among the shapes of the world.

Sound appears and then disappears; it seems trapped in time. What does sound have to do to become space? Let loose its shadow. Bounce itself around. Become larger than life itself. The echo is the first evidence most of us have that sound takes time to move through space. "Hey!" you shout across to the mountain wall. *Hay, hey, he, hi h, hss, hsss*—the sound reverberates and dissolves away. Even the small child grasps this dimension of sound. There is no echo without the shout. And every cry has its echo. A shadow in sound? A dark shape that bends the first gasp of truth into the air and back to a distant hiss? Sound cannot last long without its reminding returns through the air.

Take your ax, and go stand in the bottom of a canyon. Blow on the instrument, pluck it, strike it, let out a piercing wail. Listen to what the world gives back. Play with the response, question it, explore the sonic shape of the land.

When back inside, don't be afraid to remember. Simulate the effect; use a machine that echoes, that bounces back your tone in multifarious ways. Listen to what has been done with your sound. Decide if there's any difference between the song and its echo, the call and the response, the real and the unreal.

Sounds stay with us. They just won't quit. Thoreau reveled in the echo above his pondside retreat, for it gave him a true sense of place: "The echo is, to some extent, an original sound, and therein is the magic and charm of it. It is not merely a repetition of what was worth repeating in the bell, but partly the voice of the wood; the same trivial words and notes sung by a wood nymph." And he never forgot the whistle of civilization that came daily with the evening train.

Nevertheless, we are barraged by sounds, and so have to attune ourselves to appreciate certain ones rather than others. The katy-did's questioning *chch chch chch* and the cicada's swelling whine don't sound alike, but what does the difference mean to us? The sound of a particular kind of auto engine might take us back to a childhood vacation, just as the smell of wood smoke takes us back to a woodland cabin. The bell reminds us that recess is over years after we've left school.

Once I walked a narrow trail through the misty woods to the very tip of the Gaspé Peninsula, Cap Forillon—the Land's End of Quebec, jutting eastward into the Atlantic. At the final, fog-enshrouded cliff, a huge booming noise erupted from a foghorn, so loud that it was painful to approach too near. With hands pressed close over my ears, I walked right up to the strange noisemaking machine, and beneath it I spied a porcupine, asleep in the tall sedges. Was he deaf? Perhaps; but I think maybe he just liked the vibrations.

The warning boom at Forillon echoes out to the invisible ships at the mouth of the St. Lawrence. Who knows how far it reaches? And the echo in my mind of the sound is of the sleeping porcupine snoring in the grass, oblivious to whether anyone would remember this noise or its vast improbability. Sounds appear, and then they go. Is there no way to gather them together in memory?

Step into any one of the great cathedrals, and even the *thlack* of a footstep will reverberate for many seconds. There can be no silence in these great halls of God, as the currents of air are constantly moving, straining off the implacable stones. These acoustic edifices took hundreds of years to build, and their architects knew they were constructing fabulous echo chambers. Even in the darkness, even past eternal lights, these churches would throw sounds back and across one another, where they would fade and swell, changing space into time as the sounds changed shape, time into space as sounds found a way to last.

It has been said that these buildings were essential for the development of polyphonic music—music in which different melodies are played or sung simultaneously, resulting in a harmony. Hear the shadow in the great hall. The melody lingers, takes a while to fall. It lands gently on top of other melodies; they begin to wind together. This may be how Gregorian chant evolved into Renaissance weavings of sound, odd harmonies, strange cadences. The linger of echo may be what led all those musical rules to be established by Rameau and Fux in the Baroque period, those laws that the best composers knew how to secretly evade.

There is no obvious *need* for harmony, but the idea must have occurred to someone. Music history doesn't think too kindly of this architectural explanation, but I suspect that the insight of blending two into one was a sudden improvisation, a thought that struck as one melody shadowed another, lifting away and finally turning back again and surprising the first with a totally different answer than the delay and the repeat. It's when the echo to "Hello" is not just *hello hello hello hello* but "Goodbye" that we know someone else is actually out there.

A culture in New Guinea, the Bosavi, has a word for this kind of dance of sounds. They call it *dulugu ganalan,* "lift-up-over sounding," by which they mean that our songs and our cries gambol around the aural happenings of the natural world. But the Bosavi live in the forest. We Westerners live within boundaries we ourselves have erected. Inside our own houses we control our own echoes.

And lately, the echo has become even more abstract. We no longer need to build it in, to listen to the walls: these days we can turn it on and off with our machines. This is the most amazing myth yet of sound becoming space. Why, no budding electric guitarist can resist turning the reverb switch up to eleven. Sound can not only be much louder than life, now it can echo beyond the bounds of any real room. It can spread its wings into imaginary space.

What happens when you think of an echo as being like a shadow? Will it follow you, or will it fade away and be laid to rest? Can you move with it, or does it hold you in place? Sounds improve when their surrounding space is made audible. They seem grander, more present, seeming to emanate from some tangible space.

What music needs is a shadow to defeat time. Sounds appear and dissipate, and we wish they could last and remain, still presenting a sensible order. The echo does this, lets one sound cascade upon the next, as well as intensifying the way a single tone can fill a space, identify a hall, reveal a canyon or an amphitheater. Once we are used to hearing a sound along with its shadow, real or conjured, we cannot go back to the unadorned tone. The echoless room will seem reduced, dead, turned inward instead of embracing the world. This is where technology has intervened, why we have sound *effects;* we now turn instruments into things that do not play pure sounds but transform them, not just into music, but into imaginary spaces and worlds.

"Turn up the reverb." That's what the singer says up on stage to the soundman at the mixing board at the back of the hall during the sound check. He's like the rest of us: he would rather sing in the shower than in the dry room of reality. What good is all this echo— a sound that seems more than it is, filling up space as it bounces off the auditorium walls, off the tiles? Why does a bathroom make anyone sound better? It's because of the echo: whether real, inspired by caverns or cathedrals (or modern shower stalls), or artificial, created by electronic means, echo turns sound into the room. It makes the music last. And are *we* not the music while the music lasts?

Listen to the groovin' instrumental beginning of "Papa Was a Rolling Stone" by the Temptations and you will hear something strangely rollin' about the string parts right at the start. They rise up, swell, fade away, just like that stone, traveling through the days. The sound comes from this world but goes out of this world. It's strange and familiar at the same time. And we still remember it, all these many years later.

Reverb is phenomenological. It works at the level of the senses, affecting us before we can analyze and decide what is happening. It comes right between the performer and the listener. Edmund Husserl pointed out in *The Phenomenology of Internal Time Consciousness* that once a sound happens, it immediately goes away. Once it's over, we begin to forget it at once. That's what memory itself is, the history of forgetting. We only start etching memory into a permanent story once it is far enough gone. Tom Waits puts it more clearly than Husserl in his "operachi romantico," *Frank's Wild Years:* "Today is gray skies, tomorrow is tears. You'll have to wait 'til yesterday is here." The past is so much safer—because it isn't real and will never come? Keep waiting. It will soon be more real than today because we fix it exactly as we want it to be.

There is no way to recover the sound that once was, but reverb helps. It keeps the sound in the air, and fills the space around. It could be a real space—a cathedral, an amphitheater, or a stairwell— or the imaginary space of dreams or machines. Acousticians have written much on what makes the perfect acoustic space, and the engineers of sonic enhancement toys have worked tirelessly to simulate such spaces, but rarely have they reflected on just why we can be lured so deeply in to such simulacra. Perhaps it is because the reason is so simple: *reverb turns time into space.*

The practice rooms in the music building of the college I went to had such dead acoustics that whatever you played sounded horrendous. Either it made you want to play for hours until something halfway decent came out, or it made you give up your ax forever. Both results were common. In contrast, on the stage of the auditorium upstairs, a beautiful acoustic space, even unpracticed ensembles would benefit from the pleasing sonic ambience of the hall. Which is the more honest place to play?

No one wants to hear live music in a room with bad acoustics. It will sound like mud. Why not enhance one's sounds by a beautifully fulfilling acoustic environment? The building itself pays a compliment to the musicians. Everyone wins. It's only less "real" if you think your music belongs entirely to you. But we sing and play in a context, and music is a blend of sound that comes out into the world and immediately disappears. It's real only when played again or as it insinuates itself into our memories.

But we get our music as often on a record as in the flesh. We're used to sound seeping out from the world around, from speakers on the shelf or in the car or in the ceilings of megastores or from amplifiers connected to guitars. Music is taken for granted, part of our environment, inseparable from the machines that bring it to us with a point and a click.

As long as there has been recorded music people have tried to make it sound as large as can be. Reverb isn't just there when Jimi Hendrix discovers life in outer space, the distorted wash of his guitar receding into eternal distances; it's also what makes the sound of the Vienna Philharmonic, playing on a magnificent gilded stage, seem plausible coming out of your speakers in your room at home. The more recent the recording, the more likely it is that the sound of every single instrument is technologically enhanced.

Neither is reverb just the repeating echo of a cry across the Grand Canyon; rather, it is a complex series of echoes coming from all sides, reflecting off of different materials, at different angles, and all these differences are the stuff that computer programs make easy to manipulate—indeed, simulating reverb is one of the things that digital technology is particularly good at, so good that it's relatively easy to make things sound even better than an actual room.

We all have experienced the way some music just lingers on in the open caverns of memory. For me, those European jazz recordings on the ECM label in the seventies did that, from Keith Jarrett's crystalline close-miked piano of the Köln Concert to the chamber jazz of Ralph Towner and Jan Garbarek. Those records shimmer in space, with just a few instruments filling out a complete and enveloping sound. Each separate instrument is audible so clearly because of the way it was recorded—saxophone, twelve-string guitar, drums, bass: these instruments don't naturally mix without amplification, and only through careful artificial processing are they able to sound their best. Some call these recordings grandiose, fluffed up with too much reverb—for we all know how easy it is to lay on too much of a good thing. If the reverb is effective, though, you will barely notice it is there. You won't be able to figure it out right away, but will instead listen and say aaahhh, something about this music is filling the space all around me. It draws you out into the far reaches of the imaginary room that makes the music sound better than it could ever sound in person. And what's the problem with that? This music lives only on record—these guys will never play together again. The record is this music's true form. The live concert—in a noisy room with coughs and shuffles, an imperfect sound system, a bad seat—will almost never sound as good.

Reverb isn't passé today, but second nature. For a hundred bucks you can buy a box that does what a thousand bucks could do ten years back, in the studio or on stage: give the illusion that the sound coming out of that cheap microphone through those beer-stained Marshall speakers coated in blue glitter-foam actually originated in the proscenium of a huge Roman amphitheater. We can recreate tunnels, caverns, concert halls empty or full, large or small, bathrooms, stairwells, even a solo coming from interstellar space. It's not that we imagine we're in a different place than we are, it's just that whatever space we listen in can now gain new sonic realities.

But isn't reverb just a cheap attempt at novelty, to make something simple sound like much more than it is? We dress up the familiar in cool disguises, add some cute effects, and pretend the result is something really new. But all we have to sing are the same old songs, just louder than ever before, or enhanced with exotic rhythms, electronic sounds, or implausible echo effects from spaces impossible to build but easy to simulate. Reverb could be considered a false quest for an easy alternate to our own rough and real confusions.

"Wherever he lay his hat was his home. And when he died, all he left us was alone." If you're going to defend reverb as enhancement, you'll have to prove that sound effects are more than effects, but real aesthetic innovations. I really do believe that reverb turns time into space—an impossibility perhaps, but we all want to be the music while the music lasts and forget that our lives are anything more than the pure movements of sound through the air. Reverb casts the music into the space around us, and then it's so much easier to feel in the middle of it. Whatever kind of music you like, you probably know what it's like to be lost in it, to feel it dance all around you, to be one with the sound, and to forget what you'd been meaning to do or what's for dinner or who you have to call.

The real challenge to the call to authenticity is that this technology works so well. It no longer makes music sound merely better—more new and more alive—but it makes it sound more real than it could ever be without the machines. Today's 32-bit digital reverb, with all parameters adjustable, from decay time, early reflection delay, high and low rolloff to a myriad other sonic twists and turns, simply sounds better than the real thing. Recording in a real concert hall or church can be noisy, uneven, muddy, muffled, or just messy. The artificial reverb is so much more precise that the imaginary authenticity makes the imaginary more convincing than reality itself.

Is the shimmering recording like a hyperrealistic painting, high-definition TV, or the flat crispness of video as opposed to film? Not really. Although we adjust our gaze to *look* at the world, we cannot quickly shut our ears. Sound comes at us from all around, and our minds must make sense of all we perceive. We use the sense of sound to locate ourselves in our surroundings, and reverb plays with this sense by altering the way sound seems to move through space. We are so much more easily convinced by it, and the possibilities it embodies, not to imitate, but to twist and to create, are just beginning to be explored.

The biggest pitfall of arts that are mechanically reproduced is when they think of themselves as imitating something that is unique out there in a separate real world. It's more interesting when the tools start to *play* with the notion of truth, offering more than the unaided eye can see or ear can hear. As for reverb, don't think of it like a drug that trips up your synapses, but as an effect that can teach you how to hear more. If you take it seriously, it will sensitize you to the echoes of the wind in the trees or the waves as they crash now to your left, then right in front of you, and then to your right as the sea obliquely buffets the shore beneath your feet. Sound travels through space in all directions, and through this technology we will become ever more able to hear it.

This sound effect has to be called a success, for it goes far beyond replication *or* cheapening of something true or authentic. We humans can only bear so much reality; we get cold and bored and tired out there amid the wild din of sounds after not so long, and then we're ready to retreat to a world of simulated caverns, imaginary dream echoes, and that recording of the band played during the break that sounds so much better than the live show. But don't get cynical: all the tool does is demand that we pay more careful attention. Sonic illusion has always been a lot more than it's cracked up to be: it reveals the very magic that makes listening possible at all.

Think of the earliest sound you can remember. Ask yourself: Why have I remembered this sound for so long? How come it stays with me? Pick up an instrument and try to play it; learn from it, emulate it. Change it. What does the change do to your memory? Tape it. Has the purity of your mind's recollection been polluted by the new version stored on the machine?

Who can keep track of every reverberation, every memory triggered by sound? Music casts shadows we can hear, and others that can only be imagined or grabbed for at the edges of recollection. The sound that has been with me the longest comes from childhood nightmares, a recurring *ah ah ah ah* mantra caught in a continuous loop somewhere in the darkness. I'm four, five years old, running through the dark corridors of a city apartment seeing monsters, stumbling against the walls, running for cover. Though there was no reason to be scared, I can still conjure up the sound now, here or anywhere. It starts to send me into a trance just as the repeating tones hit a certain tempo, somewhere between the speed of a heartbeat and that of a running breath. I'm lost the moment I think of it. This sound casts a shadow far back, into memory or invention, I don't know which, and it will not leave me.

A few years ago radio producer Jim Metzner asked me to recreate that nightmare sound and rhythm of my childhood, for a program he was putting together for National Public Radio called *Sound Memories.* So I sat with the synthesizer, blending vocal and organ tones together, speeding up and slowing down the beat, looking for the exact pulse that would get me and hold me down. As I fixated on it, I felt the sound bounce off the wall and cast a shadow on the floor, bend at the door, and leave the room. In its place there was a hollow beating deep inside me, a repeating emptiness that my memories struggled to fill. I imagined the boom of a shadowy echo, as the *ah ah ah*s faded away into a rumble and hiss, the blood and the brain, the cloud of vibrations set off as I cranked the reverb dial higher and longer, as they were swallowed by the artificial din of endless feedback, mirrors of noise reflecting off each other to create an audible infinity of explosions and wails. The sounds were given space, and the space couldn't take it, and fought back in confusion. The result was infinite echo, sound refusing to disappear being left instead to endure.

The repeating thrum of the stylized breath or heartbeat. The dream sound that takes you back to the same place, inside you or out, whenever you hear it. It is a small step from dream noises to dream places. There are shadow places we return to over and over again in dreams. Why are they so exact? What are they trying to tell us? We need a location for events important in our lives, important even though they may never have happened.

I kept going back to such a place. I kept going there until I described the place and what I was listening to there. Once I wrote it down, I've never found it again. I may think I know the road, but the house doesn't seem to be there anymore. Does it matter? It scares me to perform this piece; I've done it only a few times. The first was at a conference, strangely enough, in the Nugget Hotel in Reno. Tony Bennett was playing downstairs. The event in the real place was dreamlike enough, though the story has me searching for another place I doubt I'll ever find:

I met the other late last night.
She was a light in the attic window.
She was a wind through the leaves
She was a house I'd been to before.

I passed the house many times on the road.
And I knew I had been there.
And I knew something happened.
But I couldn't place it, it always seemed closed.
Windows sealed up, padlocks on the door.
I began to think I had been there in dreams.

Each time I'd smile: I've been here before.
Been inside.
Something important happened in there.
Deep inside.

And I'm dancing with you by the shores of the river
And I feel another one pull me away.
She slips so silently up through the shadows
She grabs for my turns in the air.

In that house I pleaded
In that house I wouldn't let go
It was in that house that she sent me away
To watch from the sidewalk
To gaze from the darkness.
To never quite learn to say no.

But you know I'm not sure if I've actually been there
I can't tell if that house is for real.
It's not where we lived. It's not where we met.
I may never have seen it by day.

I want to have seen it, I wish it were true.
That place where all lost things are found

I visit this house only sleeping in dreams.
And it's always the same—
She's never there
She's never on time
By the time she gets there I'm gone. . . .

When we're riding together and I see our reflection
Sometimes she glares from the lake in the sun.
Or I look in accidental photos
and she seems to be back of the lens

And she pulls and she tugs
Like there's no other chance
And she drags me back into the fray.

I was there once, I know.
Or maybe not.
We make ourselves up as we go.

There was this house.
It all happened there.
Just as I willed it to be.

It has no walls.
It's more like an outline
a sketch of a cube on a plane
One less dimension
One less opportunity

I'll take it. *I'll go.*
That's it. I'm there.

Who is this other? It's not me, but a person inside me. A woman who never arrives. Or someone I'm always missing, can't quite find. Or not a person, just the dark opposite of whatever I'm supposed to stand for myself. It's a mystery making sense only in the shadow world of deep dark nights far off in the past. Maybe it's better simply to recite dreams than to be vexed by their interpretation.

Why do we have to hear things we like again and again? Same reason to return over and over again to imaginary places that we've never actually been to. To check out their outlines, fill in the blanks, turn the shadow into something whole and detailed. But how can we be specific about the hollows left by sound? They are not silences, but shadows.

I do not want to fool the ear with illusion, but to hear what is actually there. Sound never stands still, however, frozen and motionless. It appears to us only as it has already left us, and it keeps leaving, like the light from those fabulously distant galaxies that has only now arrived in our field of view, four million or more years after it left its source.

Illusion, in the end, always fails. Someone is listening out there, far away, someplace in the future, for the shadows of sounds that we have already forgotten. The music still refuses to last.

As music is played, it alights upon shadows. Perhaps the dark marks on the page are some of those shadows, since notation, once intended as a mnemonic aid for sparking memories of melodies that resided in the head, has now become the vehicle for legitimizing the smooth flow of sounds. But the musician is needed to lift the notes from the page and into the air, where, even as they dissipate, they strain not to be forgotten. The notes remind us of what should be played, while what actually comes out is fluid, uncapturable. Notes are just one aspect of music, the aspect that can be written down. A shadow of the real thing, and an imperfect shadow at that. They are imperfect because they do not move as the sound does which cast it—as it turns a corner or moves away.

Music that is not written down has another kind of shadow. Any improvising musician will tell you that practice does not make perfect, but it does help you discover that you can play things you previously believed to be impossible. An idea arrives, you hear something in the background, you respond, and you don't know why or how, except that you've been preparing for this moment, preparing for any moment, your whole musical life of listening and playing, not just following the sounds, but twisting them together with your own voice so that meaning comes out.

You might record on tape or disk such moments and then listen back and try to analyze them, try to write the action down and repeat it, only to find that although you might be able to repeat what first came spontaneously, the music will never be the same. Once practiced, repeated, learned, it becomes a shadow of its original self. Music should never lose its spontaneity; a piece should sound as if it is being offered to the world for the first time, fresh, new, confident, and tentative at once, above all alive, unplanned, following no script.

The greatest and most enduring music sounds new and familiar at the same time. It defies division into one thing or another. The whole song that you hear must be impossible to describe, a shadow of words, an outline of the truth.

All these attitudes—wandering connections, beginning the ultimate note, ending it, noticing its absence—prepare us to consider the whole world around us as a vast musical composition, which no one is solely in charge of. We can all find our place, we can all improvise a way in. But first we have to be ready and able to listen to the world as a soundscape, to all that surrounds us as some vast symphony that includes all possible symphonies. No one can write it, no one can remember it all. Every single song is one shadow of the whole.

A SENSE OF SOUNDSCAPE

Some say music is the universal language. This couldn't possibly be true. Not everyone speaks it, not all understand it. And even those who do cannot explain what it says. No one knows how music speaks, what tales it tells, how it tugs at our emotions with its mixture of tones, one after another, high and low.

You can be moved by music and have absolutely no idea why. Language is not like that. You must be able to speak a language to know what is being said. Music is only in part a language: the part you understand when you learn its rules and how to bend those rules. But the rest of it may move us even though we are unable to explain why.

The word *nature* can have many musical meanings, as well as many linguistic meanings. It can mean the place we came from, some original, ancient home where, as Nalungiaq the Netsilik Eskimo reminds us, "people and animals spoke the same language." Not only have we lost that language, but we can barely imagine what it might be. Words are not the way to talk to animals. They'd rather sing with us—if we learn their tunes without making them conform to ours. Music could be a model for learning to perceive the world by listening, not just by naming or explaining.

For to know and to feel the meaning of music are two different things. We may not know why the coyote is howling, or have any idea why the brown thrasher sings nearly two thousand songs— so many more than any other bird. But we can hear these sounds, whose meanings are not intended for us, as if they were music and soon call them beautiful. This is part of music's power.

Music links us more closely to the reverberations of the surrounding world. As soon as you begin to pay attention, the borders between things become less clear. Some compositions mirror the workings of nature *in their manner of operation,* an aesthetic dream most often attributed to John Cage. Cage learned of it from the art historian Ananda Coomaraswamy, who had extracted it from Aristotle's vision of *techne,* a word that once meant both "art" and "tool." Addressing nature as a manner of operation, we complete processes that have been left unfinished, utilizing the ingenuity that so marks human presence on the earth.

Still, with or without the human impulse to organize and perceive it, no music can exist without the given ways that sound behaves.

At the same time, music seems to be about little else besides itself —the play of tones up and away, the game of noise and silence.

Once I rode eastward out of Reykjavik on a jacked-up bus with huge balloon tires, over moraines and outflows from a great glacier in southern Iceland. My companion, Elias Davidsson, was a former orchestral composer who now makes music by banging on stones collected from the far corners of his country. "Many people collect stones," he remarked, "but usually they choose those that look or feel a certain way. I instead go for the *sound*. I hold the rock up in the air. I suspend it from wires or strings. Then I strike it with mallets or with other stones, building xylophones of strange complexity. This is the music I make out of my country."

A party was under way when we arrived at the tiny stone hut in which we would live for several days. Twenty farmers and their families had walked over the glacier from the other side, a journey of several days. They were members of a choir that had been formed by one of the farmers: crippled years before and no longer able to work the land, he had decided to bring music to his isolated village. Now the group had carried him over the mountains to this hut to celebrate their tenth anniversary.

The music was loud, boisterous, and billowing with a midsummer joy. The sun never went down, and never came up; rushing clouds and fog blowing steadily off the ice filled the persistently gray sky. I pulled out my clarinet, the instrument that comes with me wherever I go—and the reason for carrying it everywhere suddenly became clear. There is music all over the world, resounding from inside mountain shacks, echoing off melting ice and tumultuous rivers. I don't consider all of it to be good, but this was one of those moments worth traveling so far to experience, to hear.

The music I yearn for comes out of nature but sounds as if it were from a world far from home. There is a virtue in finding a song that moves from the familiar into the unfamiliar, for in this way miracles arise out of the everyday. I once heard Indian *santur* master Shivkumar Sharma play in a vast auditorium. The sound system went dead, and because his instrument, a refined hammer dulcimer, is extremely quiet, the huge crowd had to sit in utter silence to pick up even the faintest strains of his raga improvisations. The drums and the drone became so imperceptibly soft, no one dared move, lest the slightest noise obscure the beautiful sound experiments.

Sitting as quietly as possible, listening carefully for faint expressions, the whole audience had learned suddenly to hear in a new way. The music had released us into hearing nature for what it is: a vast unstoppable music, what Canadian composer Murray Schafer calls a *soundscape*—as inescapable for us as the landscapes that enable us to stand out from and also be a part of them. Sounds define us, hold us in, lead us away. They announce themselves to us, they call from all over the world.

It is no great challenge to hear all sounds as music—this is the culmination of musical history. In the twentieth century, classical musicians broke the rules of harmony to welcome chance as well as noise into the mix of organized sound. Popular musicians, seeking ever more variation within accessible constraints, have sampled beats, noises, whirrs, and chirps from all available sources. And jazz musicians have improvised over sound changes as well as chord changes. If music is progressing anywhere, it is toward a blurring of boundaries, toward what ethnomusicologist Steven Feld calls a "schizophonia," where it is impossible to know where any sound is coming from or what it might musically mean.

The eighteenth-century composer Antonio Vivaldi wrote a "Goldfinch" Concerto in which the flutists are supposed to play in a manner reminiscent of a goldfinch. And in the twentieth century, Olivier Messiaen meticulously transcribed birdsongs and required that the orchestra play them note for note. Today we might jam with birds or play their sounds directly out of black-box machines. Modernity in music has prepared us to accept sound merely as sound, with harmonic rules having been bent and twisted so much that they finally fall away. This is no culmination, only a beginning of a cross-cultural journey that will in no time have us concerting with kookaburras and flamingos as a matter of course. Life sings and improvises from molecules to galaxies. Sound speaks to us, yet has nothing specific to tell. The melodies of the world are what they are. Nothing less, nothing more. You should never be afraid to *listen.*

Nature need not be the nightingale stuck in a cage who will only sing if a cloth is drawn around its bars. We will not survive as artists or as a species if we cannot become part of the world that surrounds us. There should be no duality between music and nature. Natural sound is never clearly separable from human sound. The moment we decide to listen, to seek out meaning, we start to change the world. We cannot preserve that sound world apart from our listening, nor can we make music without sensing its resonance in an environment, be it a concert hall, a bedroom, a car, a bar, or a windy bluff out in the rain.

Nature sound specialist Bernie Krause has written that no recording technology can "capture" nature. The microphone is merely a tool for making artifacts out of sound. These, like our visual images, are immediately transformed into something human. In his collected poems *No Nature,* Gary Snyder reminds us that "we do not easily know nature," adrift in sound play between *no* and *know.* But there can be no humanity without the surrounding nature that has made us possible. Although we imagine we have free will, an environment is necessary for our survival. We are bounded, enjoyed, devoured, by the world. We owe it respect and involvement.

How might music come to resemble nature only in its "manner

of operation"? Many of us are attracted to Cage's idea but are unsure just what it means. Perhaps we are drawn to it because as artists we want our works to be integrated enough to approach the *necessity* that is nature, a nature that might not be perfect but is something that seems essential, fitting into the world so precisely. If we create a work that becomes something the world could not possibly do without, then we have succeeded in being necessary to the world around us. This might be easy for other living creatures, but it is paradoxically difficult for human beings.

For, while we are created from nature, we are also cast out by our wily, cultured ways. And that is why we experience the perennial aesthetic pull of the earthy, the natural, the green, the living. Of course, nature is more than life. It is death, eternity, calamity, softness, and devastation. Some say there is no evil in nature, that all violence is tempered by some kind of endless balance. Others maintain that humanity finds what it wishes in the malleable environment, that a naturalistic aesthetics is only a matter of projection. I disagree with both these views. There are real powers out there, whether inside a bird call or thunderclap. It may mean nothing to hear a chirp and be able to identify its avian source: that's just order and classification. It takes dwelling inside an ecology, however, to know the *significance* of a wayward sound. To hear each noise as a melody in a vast improvisation, the enveloping soundscape that makes up this world, is the final task of the attentive listener. Once trained to listen, you will let the sounds and their significance find you, not just hear what you are listening for.

This is not a nature with no place for humanity. If our sounds fit in, *we* can fit in. Even though today's nature-sounds recordists complain that there is hardly a place in the United States where the thrum of jet engines doesn't interrupt wild soundscapes, no less attentive a listener than Thoreau enjoyed hearing the bells peal over his beloved Walden. "Over the woods this sound acquires a certain vibratory hum, as if the pine needles in the horizon were the strings of a harp which it swept. All sound heard at the greatest possible distance produces one and the same effect, a vibration of the universal lyre." Increasing our listening acumen makes the world more alive, with beautiful juxtapositions, ironies, hums, songs, whirrs, blusters, rips, rolling waters, and suns searing the horizon to a crisp. Sounds crackle through the inaudible airwaves, a choir of life and death, eternal geologic rumblings.

We react immediately to sound, but we do not trust it to offer information: although we hear where things come from, we must see them to know what they are. We cannot close our ears, yet we do not adjust our hearing the way we refocus our gaze. This is why music—by teaching us to enjoy what we hear—might be an avenue toward appreciating ecology, as visual acuity allows us to look outward upon the world we claim. If we treat each sound as part of a meaningful sonic world, the natural world might resound more like the home that it is.

What is the difference between a human sound and a natural one? I used to think it was easy to discern the *whoom* of a machine from the call of an animal. But then I heard the monotonous, even-toned *ping* of the northern saw-whet owl in a wintry Canadian forest—a high, tinny note that can repeat evenly for hours on end— and I knew that a living creature could sound just like a machine. Or the tinny *whee-urp* of the red-bellied woodpecker, a bird with a red head but a brown belly, living high in local hardwood trees, almost impossible to see. The sound is instantly distinctive, but it sounds mechanical, planned out, regular and exact. Now, does a sound become more potent if I know who is making it? No. Identification of species isn't the same as real listening. We have to feel these sounds, internalize them, turn them into inspiration for improvisation, so that we may naturally fit in to the surrounding world.

Go outside. Listen carefully with open ears. Pick one sound, pay attention only to it. Describe it carefully, either in words or in a picture. Then think about the sound, its structure, its effect on you. Pick up your instrument, and try to play something inspired by that one sound. Don't just imitate it, but learn from it. Feel how it works, turn it into a music that is shaped by what you have heard and understand. Hear if you've managed to fit in, if you've made any difference to the world at all.

Living or nonliving, sonic images can help us work like nature. Sound shapes are never exact, only suggestive; are not fixed, but are always subtly moving. Sudden noises have a natural fullness, a richness that surpasses the bleeps of machines. There may be a repetitive minimalism out there in the world, but it ebbs and flows; it is rarely pounding and incessant, but is rocking, varying, never the same.

Of course, learning to expertly record and appreciate the sounds of nature is not the same as making music out of nature. Some ways of combining sounds seem to make living, breathing artworks, but that is not always the case. Not all music moves close to nature, and not all natural sound is music.

Music is in a great sense in the ear of the beholder. If you listen well enough, any series of sounds can have the organization and quality necessary for it to be knowable and lovable as music. That is what artistic abstraction has offered us in the twentieth century: openness to the beauty of the world in newly direct ways.

Music heard in nature or made out of nature is any series of sounds that can be appreciated for their depth, beauty, and artistry. These include wind voices and whale songs, as well as people playing in forests, canyons, concert halls, and stairwells. Any music that fits into its place, is enhanced by its surroundings and not fighting against them, is an environmental music. The sound out there is music if you can hear it as a beautiful form to be enjoyed in itself apart from what it is intended to accomplish.

David Ignatow's most famous poem says simply, "I should be content to look at a mountain for what it is and not as a comment on my life." Those words have haunted me for years, and they suddenly come back to me now as I wonder what the sound of, say, waves crashing on a fine Pacific sand beach really are—just a wash of water that comes to land again and again, or unbelievably sweet music that has no beginning and will never end? Which of these is the comment on *my* life? Which is the world in itself? This is the classic question of the phenomenologist, the seeker of a message from the world that precedes interpretation. Again, what can you make of the songs of birds before dismissing them with the mere name of the singer. Say "green-winged warbler," and most people leave it at that. But what of the *sound*—where does it take you? What of the sound of surf pounding the shore? It cannot be easily reduced to a recording. What does it mean to truly hear it?

That beach sound is elusive. Emulations like Mendelssohn's *Fingal's Cave* Overture—da da dada *dah* dom, played over and over again to suggest the magnificence of the wavy sea—cannot capture it. He turned the rhythmic quality of the sea into a musical guide, and it works to a point, but something about it makes the sea less than it actually is. Instead, we can learn to hear the waves themselves as music, to welcome the surf into our realm of possible art and work with it, learn from it, build on it.

I have said nothing about the important role music can and does play as propaganda for nature: people recording and performing songs that praise nature and protest what humanity is doing to the environment. Music can be instrumental in human transformation, though in this case the music is too easily deemed to be of quality simply because of the good it does. How dare one say something bad about any music that serves so good a cause? But if we are afraid to talk about what is good or not good in a work of art, then we cannot instill standards against which such works might be measured. The melody and rhythm, skillfully done, will bring the message alive, keep it moving and current; indeed, the best of this music transforms the message into something that can be conveyed no other way.

In the midst of the environmental crisis perpetuated by humanity, all artists, including musicians and composers, can find ways to make constructive contributions to solutions, in part by insisting on excellence in their own work. It is not only the aesthete who wants a better music that draws from the sounds and structures of nature. Those of us who wish our species to care more for the environment will not achieve our goal by stating scary facts and feeling guilt at the damage we have wrought. We're used to *seeing* the devastating effects of humanity upon nature, from the sludging of rivers to the smogging of the sky. But we can *hear* what's awry just as easily: Where are all the songbirds who used to live here? Can we find no place free from the droning sounds of human creation? All over the planet, peace is disrupted by distant jet airplanes, grinding chainsaws. That's simply the way we live.

But music didn't cause this trouble. Music is an art that moves stealthily onward, tying humanity to the rhythms of the world. Despite my emphasis here on making art out of sound—cutting and pasting, rendering virtual sound-pictures on tape and on disk, recording events that never happened—it is much more important to get out there and jam, to play with the world and let the world play with us.

The flutist Michael Pestel and I have gone right into the National Aviary in Pittsburgh to jam in person with real-live birds, from ground cuckoos to laughing thrushes. Some of these birds really get into it, jump right up to the flute, enjoying themselves, listening eagerly, joining in. Other musicians are out there in the wilderness jamming with whales and wolves—though if we know about it, it's usually because it's been put down on tape, perhaps tinkered with to step up a specific effect: a wild encounter changed through technology into an object. Still, that's more direct than extracting precious bits of nature to insert into our own artificial sound worlds. If we use nature, we must really listen and put sounds to work in a way that respects nature's own life and integrity—to the extent possible.

There is also music that seems to *live* just by the way it moves, and by how it draws the listeners and players closer together around a common, organic pulse. Musicologist (he prefers his own term, "muse-echologist") Charles Keil calls this the *groove* and has written that the best music grooves take us up into their world, holding a part of us there even after the sound has ceased. It's the thrum of life, the catchy beat, the pattern that the drummer and woodpecker can share.

Buckminster Fuller was fond of pointing out that although pop music seems to get faster and faster, people still are able to keep dancing to it. There has always been room for both the quick and the languorous in the way people can move to a beat. Was earlier music any more natural because the tools that made it were more simple? It's tempting to view that old musical life of gathering together, playing together, making art together as being closer to nature. But the expanding of our listening acceptance and the imitative powers of our machines have led some people to claim that electronic music is closer to the whirr and thrum of the world in process than anything humans could make previously. More and more people dance to machine-generated beats, swearing that these sounds are more hypnotic than what people can play on acoustic instruments. Maybe so, maybe so. It is true that human-made musical instruments may make up the best of our machines. From drums and didgeridoos to euphoniums and theremins, the enhancement of human expression is surely one of our greatest achievements.

This idea supports the aesthetic principle that something can be good if it *sounds like* nature. And if it's especially good, it will change the way we hear nature, define nature, and then live in nature. Hopefully the trajectory of Western culture has taught us to hear more, not less, and to hear enough that we begin to question the entire course of that culture. By listening, by dancing, by grooving, we can make music itself an agent for change.

Music poised for the uncertainties of life and able to change its direction in unexpected situations calls attention to the inadequacy of inflexible human plans. There is an "earth jazz" that is more a philosophy of living than it is a music: improvising with nature; offering designs like chord changes, structures that may be bent by new opportunities offered by circumstance. If we jam with the world with the same intelligence and awareness as a skilled jazz musician, we stand a chance of learning a way into the great improvised complexity of the natural world, a concert so immense and endless that we may never be humble enough to accept our role in it.

For humanity will always be but a small part of the world's music, and there will always be many more structures and forms for us to discover and learn inside this vast mélange of sound. These structures serve only to guide, not to replace aural experience. You can love music and be touched by it even if you know no music theory. That's why calling music a language is only going after a small part of its power.

So does nature "understand" music? The world is full of beings who listen along with us. We'll never know how they comprehend what they hear. We people have invented many categories to explain the extent of our world, and its bounds, yet we can do so only because we occupy a place in a natural world, an enveloping place that always sounds a little different when we listen differently. There is a "natural" harmonic series that came from the overtones of wind in the trees before, a few thousand years ago, Pythagoras plucked it out on a single string. It can be easily heard in guitar harmonics, and on ancient instruments the world over that capitalize on this natural behavior of sound: Aeolian harps left to resonate in coastal winds; overtone flutes with no fingerholes that play up and down the series, somehow approximating the blues, which endures because it is neither major not minor but in some essential untempered place in between; the harmonic throat-singing of the Asian steppes from Tibet to Tuva, where one human voice can sing several pitches at once, all natural resonances, somehow complete and rousing.

The natural harmonic series is not arbitrary, but rather a confluence between the way sound behaves and the range of the human ear. Again, our physical properties bind us inextricably to nature: our perception of music derives from the way we hear the wind in the trees. Other creatures might come up with musics that we are unable to hear; there might be entirely different ranges of music in nature that we are simply unaware of. Not only can we hope to discover what ours is meant to be, but we can also expand the range of our hearing by magnifying differences we might otherwise never hear. Amplification can be one tool for increasing sensitivity, as long as we don't abuse or overuse it.

Music can help us discover the limits of nature by giving us newly creative ways of fitting into the surrounding world. This is true of many kinds of music that could be called "environmental"—ones that create worlds, places to move into. Brian Eno, for example, wants his music "not to evoke landscape, but to *be* landscape." These are pieces with no beginning or end, constituting worlds you can enter and then leave when you wish. They work if they have as much integrity as a landscape, and as much necessity. It's a good landscape if you want to spend more time inside it, exploring, walking, living in it as if you belong there.

Is that too placid? Nature, after all, can be frightening, dangerous, and unbearable too. Do we want only sweet soundscapes? Of course not. But we probably want sound worlds that seem intelligent, infinitely various, endlessly interesting. As a listener you will always be able to choose. So look for fresh criteria with which to assess this new kind of music. Don't accept it uncritically.

That's the human plight all over again: To come from nature and then to have to work so hard to get back to it. It's an endless adventure. It keeps our species alive, but it also keeps us dangerous.

There is music in nature and nature in music. Isn't it wonderful that we can love and be immersed in both without needing to understand how the two are intertwined? It is enough to know that they are.

The sense of sight usually provides the most details, at least of the kind we can enumerate. Scent has a powerful ability to spur recollection, to arouse memories of being enveloped in different places in the past. Touch suggests our body's presence and limits. And sound gives an impression of our environment: what is around us, where we fit in. This is its immediate contribution to ecology.

Psychologist Abraham Maslow said, "Don't let the noise bother you": self-realization means independence from those forces around you that are out of your control. But an ecological sense of self means folding in to what's around, to hear it before it hears you, to be welcomed into the surroundings rather than pretending they don't matter. Music may be made out of nature or reflect the workings of nature, but how does a stronger sense of sound improve us, rather than disturbing us? Think first of those sound worlds that lie clear in memory, that have significance whenever you recall them.

First: a sudden shift to silence. When the float plane left me behind on Lake Komaktorvik in northern Labrador, what I was least prepared for was the utter silence. No noise moved in this arctic world, and the immediate stark feeling was of a nature where humankind had no place, where we were strange interlopers. Forget everything about this remarkable place but the sound, a cleansing emptiness, a purity that won't stay separate, not at all. I think of the blue sky, the contorted wild mountain shapes rising into the fog, the taste of the utterly perfect water untainted even by a recent human glance. This is the stillness of the arctic, the wilderness repose. Hold on to it, knowing that in minutes the world could roar and rain and wind could pelt your face from the tumultuous sky. This tranquillity transcends all artifice. It was *out there,* not in the mind. It's out there still.

Then: wind rustling Colorado aspens. *Quaking,* they call it, a fluttering of light and dark and then the nearly white-noise rush of billowing wind on leaves. I am standing on a lonely autumn road. Hitchhiking. Waiting for that warm *whoosh* of a speeding car, to hear it screech to a halt, a ride out of there. A time-bound soundscape, with anticipation, nature, and the road out, a need to get somewhere. Yet I remember the waiting. Never refuse wind, or its memory.

Further memories: the intense complexities of wave against dark, fine sand. Whooshing from the left, then from the right, hitting the beach obliquely and still thundering down, indescribable, irreducible, a booming pattern that only approximates rhythm. It has no rhythm itself, but it inspires rhythm, it conspires to fill all frequencies into our ears. *Da da dade dah dom.* This sound is deep inside but easy to thrust up to the surface of recall. I replay it in my head through the steady drone of fans and air conditioners contriving to keep me artificially cool now, at this moment. The waves, though close by, are elusively imaginary. They cannot be recorded or replaced or easily written down. Yet they are infinitely stimulating, contain infinite music. That is the perfection in the waves.

Not far from my house there is an open but lush wood. Thrushes call to one another high in the canopy, impossible to see but impossible to ignore. A birdsong is not a bird call. The latter is a brief shout, an announcement, while the former is music, a song for the joy of it, an affirmation whose need science cannot and really does not want to explain.

There is no *reason* for the complexity of birdsongs, no excuse for their beauty. Birds are composers, performers, and improvisers. Although ornithologists are impressive when they can immediately match a species with its sound, is not something lost when the magic tones quickly have a name? They may know what the bird is, but not why its song is the way it is. How best to inhabit a bird's song, its place in the trembling soundscape? Play with it, respond to it, try (in vain) to imitate it. Listen to it, let it inspire you, try to feel it flowing into all other senses. Describe it in completely other terms.

Think how hard it is to describe the "abstract" sounds of birds in words. The *peooh, peooh, pemh, pemn* of the cardinal, a discrete, crisp, song like the clear, sudden flash of its astonishing red against rustling green leaves. Old Sam Peabody Peabody Peabody is supposed to be the white-throated sparrow, but it doesn't speak words: it whistles high and clear, *doo peeh peeeuuwee, peeuuwee, peeeuuwee.* But that's not it either. No words can express what a creature says in sounds that are so clearly alien from our phrasing or our writing or even our music. To learn a song, you need not know the name of a bird, but you must start to inhabit its rhythm and color, you must find a way to come at its qualities from inside, not outside.

We know so little for sure about the natural world! Think of the most beguiling example of animals producing enigmatic, musical sounds. Before the late 1960s and the invention of the hydrophone, an underwater microphone, human beings didn't even know whales could sing. When Roger Payne and Scott McVay first dropped their hydrophones into the water and heard the astonishing sounds of humpback whales, they entered a state of awe. "I heard the size of the ocean that night," writes Payne. "As if I had walked into a dark cave to hear wave after wave of echoes cascading back from the darkness beyond. The cave spoke to me. That's what whales do, give the ocean its voice." And that's what humanity can do as well through music: give the whole planet a voice. But it should be a voice marked by sensitivity and humility.

We can learn this sensitivity, this humility, by increasing our attentiveness to the sounds around us. Find your way inside the musical sensibilities of birds, of whales, of the cicadas in the trees. Much of the literature on whale songs tries to demonstrate that whale vocalizations have qualities similar to human music: identifiable rhythms, themes and variations, phrases that make sense in human time as well as whale time. But must music fit human patterns if it is to be called music? Why not learn from the whale world, rather than attempting to sync it into ours? This is the greatest challenge of learning from nature: taking it on its own terms.

Experts say that when we listen to whale songs we slow down. We ease into rhythms that change very slowly, we get a sense of being far inside the deep, inside a sound world where the beats and squeaks travel for hundreds of miles. Katy Payne discovered that whales not only compose, but they *improvise,* tinkering with their songs in subtle ways that the whole pod gradually latches on to, such that one season they're all singing one song, the next season another, a chorus of similarity that evolves through creative foray. How and why does the change happen? No one knows. How do whales make their sounds? Again, amazingly, no one knows. But we do know enough to listen, and to reach out for guidance if we're willing to try another species' rules. Doing so will most certainly change us, just as I was changed by gradually entering the sound world of the Tibetan gyaling in that monastery on the other side of the world.

Just as music links together cultures that cannot talk to each other, it may allow us to reach out to species we are unable to ask questions of in any other way. Jim Nollman has spent years playing music to whales—not composing with their sounds, but improvising directly with them, often on electric guitar beamed underwater. It's no easier than working with human musicians; you never know when they'll show up. "Start off playing quietly," he writes.

> Treat the music as an invitation. Visualize the bond of time and place as a sanctuary filled with music. Feel what it means to get on whale time. Don't try to communicate; remain humble to the fact that music —especially "beautiful music"—is a judgment call. That rare bird known as the interspecies musician learns to meet the animal halfway, two species willing to play in the same band, if but for a moment. It frolics with our basic conception of what it means to be both human and animal.

If you listen to a soundscape while in the midst of it, expect pulses, flows, shadows, and light like the wind in the trees, the crash of the ocean, the slide of a mountain crumbling into rubble after an earthquake. Be like an animal, or like a whole living watershed. What kind of human culture can fit into all this? Maybe you hear people gathering in from the forest and singing, dancing, teaching, and playing, all together in a rush of tension and release.

Edward S. Curtis in 1915 described how a Kwakiutl "song-maker" derives his music from the sound of a waterfall. First, he sits beside the water and gently hums along. A roll of sounds appears to him: *hamamama.* That's the theme he begins with, tossing it around on his tongue, testing the rhythms, developing a form. His assistant, called the "word-passer," joins in, *hamamama, hamamama,* and then tests a single word along with the rhythm, say, *fish.* And then he bends the word *fish, fishhhhshhhhshhh,* above the *hamamama,* and listens for other sounds to apply to the source to bend it further.

A ratcheting kingfisher skims the surface of the river, piercing its beak downward for the kill. Look at the pattern the bird leaves on the water after it spears its prey. So quickly gone. Remember it, in melody or song. Ask those around you to help. Make the music together and blend it in with the surrounding sounds. Scoop up the melody from the world in your hands.

Nature is no background, no fixed sea on which to musically sail. For its sounds too can be moved around, arrayed into patterns— repeating ones, new ones, inflections up and down. Many collage pieces have been made out of the sounds of the environment, of course, but they have been rarely played in the moment, improvised coolly and carefully. In the work I've done with the sound designer and composer Douglas Quin, who has recorded exotic and endangered natural sounds all over the planet, I have encouraged him not just to make tapes, but to play along live, as an improviser in touch with the moving soundscape. The orchestra of natural sounds played by either keyboard or guitar through a sampler takes the synthesizer to the next step in music: it plays the earth directly, rather than simply emulating it the way music traditionally has done.

But for this kind of playing to work, we have to learn to listen to the environment, to its sounds. We will have to tackle hard questions of what is good and bad in the aesthetics of nature, and not ignore, in Zen fashion, our likes and dislikes. We must push toward the universal good by artistically defending what we do, by showing in the art itself why and how it works, and not fall sway to easy exoticism.

Listen to a crowd of walruses beating their tusks on the rocks, making a rhythm, a drum circle, a song of purpose. And what about those whale songs? Have we really understood them musically, or have we just inserted them into our standard forms as suddenly new effects, ornamental twists upon what we already know?

The philosopher Theodor Adorno didn't especially like jazz because he thought it was not genuinely innovative. What passed for an improvised solo, he charged, was really just a trivial variation on the familiar: one still had to stay within the changes, and never break the rules. He missed the point of the music, but his critique still hits home: when the art is genuinely new, we are uncertain how to accept it. The radical cannot ride the familiar. What Adorno said counts for a lot of popular music today, which exhibit the same old forms and turns of phrase, but with new sounds substituted for the old—the synthesizer instead of the string section, the techno drumbeat instead of the rock-solid drummer at the set.

Making music that works like nature cannot follow easy conventions, because our musical rules have lost track of the fluid dance cycles of the earth. The pulse of nature has no beginning, middle, or end. Natural music must similarly attune us to rhythms that are always in play, constant trances that we tune into when we wish, tune out of as we step away, though they keep on going beyond the borders of our minds and bodies. We plan the music only enough that we can be taken further than we think possible: playing, listening, dancing, using the beat to feel at home.

If you want your art to help humanity *fit in* to a nature that, as poet A. R. Ammons puts it, "has brought us this far but then cast us out," then you will want to create not only things or experiences that live, but works that are themselves like landscapes, places to return to again and again. This doesn't mean the music will thrive simply as a background for your life, although that's what many of us use music for, a soundtrack to keep spinning so that we forget just how empty they are. No, these musics as landscapes can also be listened to as *examples* of how we might live differently in the world, as models of a way of living and moving where all breathes together and where one part does not fight against the other parts. The sounds move, the minds move, the bodies move. The music makes you dance inside.

Think of placing your music in a forest. It should evoke the forest but not compete with the forest. It should allow the forest, or make possible the forest, or, best, make necessary the forest, or have the forest really need it so that the land becomes a better place because of the music and not in spite of it. Or record the sound of a river. Listen to it, swim in it, sing inside it, figure out how to add to the burbling so you might make it more than it is without you listening, playing. The river does not hear itself as music. We, as musicians, must change our understanding of music so that it encompasses the voice of the river. Then we may expand our discipline of improvisation so that we can play along with it and embrace it as more than trivial effect.

I imagine a world of music-making and listening where we perceive the din of our surroundings with precise and pleasurable attention. Where each birdsong amazes us, where every peal of thunder is like a word from above, its message exact. We will converse with the world again. People and stones will speak the same language, recalling that old Eskimo memory of the wonder of ancient days. Only it won't quite be like a language: it will be like music. You won't need to have mastery of it to love it. Just hearing it will be enough to draw you in. It will be one thing to appreciate this language, and another to understand it, to figure out. Like the difference between simply *playing* music and learning its principles, its theory. One does not need both. In fact, explanation has been known to stop the creation.

We will be immersed in a whole world that can be heard as a vast musical composition. The idea has certainly been around for a long time, at least since the futurists with their bold manifestos of noise-music, factory symphonies, and rousing contrapuntal choirs issuing from the rising clamor of the last century. For this call to listen and *enjoy* is not necessarily tied to nature, nor is it especially environmental. It might just be a strategy to learn to love noise instead of thinking of it as pollution.

Art's primary purpose is to show us beautiful and wondrous ways of making something new out of the old, familiar materials of the world. Or to comment on what's happening in a poignant, unique way that no scientific explanation can replace. The work comes first, then comes a way for the people to get to it. If it is successful, it changes the way we experience things, how we live in a world where so much cries out to be seen, heard, felt.

All this suggests why we can never truly know nature, despite that fact that it is "out there," surrounding us, waiting to be known. For we are always changing what we find as we look at it, as we hear it. The first "environmental" piece I created, *In the Rainforest,* was motivated by that one idea: that human perception of the natural world transforms it anew. The jungle becomes whatever we make of it, and from the first moment it is imagined to be comprehensible, it is already in danger. From there we may see it as the enemy, or as a home, and at last as the final resource required for the earth's survival.

The text comes from the account of a scientist seeking answers in the rich realm of diversity that the jungle reveals. When I asked E. O. Wilson, whose introductory biology class I once took at Harvard, if he would mind if I chopped up his well-written essay on the experience of observing insects in the equatorial rainforest to use as a framework for a work of music, he was surprisingly encouraging. "This," he wrote me, "is the kind of request every teacher dreams of." I suspect that rather few scientists are open-minded enough to accept the transformation of their work in this way.

The piece is constructed around certain issues: The scientist first narrows his attention, then listens and looks for patterns in the strange lush world that surrounds him. He looks for order, wishing to interpret the environment as an "organic machine." But this is an ambivalent idea, for can machines be truly animate? In the piece, improvised electronic lines and rhythms are treated as building blocks, blended together to produce sounds that seem to live, that do not simplify the world but let us revel in its complexity.

Is such study any different from the first glance? The rainforest will be whatever we make of it, though it began as something more. That is its tragedy.

1

I narrowed the world down to the span of a few meters.
The effect was strangely calming.
Breathing and heartbeat diminished, concentration intensified.
It seemed to me that something extraordinary in the forest
lay very close to where I stood,
moving to the surface and to discovery.

2

I willed animals to materialize, and they came erratically into view.
Metallic-blue mosquitoes floated down from the canopy,

black carpenter ants sheathed in recumbent golden hair
filed in haste through moss on a rotting log.
I turned my head slightly and all of them vanished.
I was a transient of no consequence in this familiar yet deeply alien
    world I had come to love.

3

What do you think of as you reach inside?
The answer is that I open an ant colony as I would
the back of a Swiss watch.
I am enchanted by the intricacy of its parts and the clean, thrumming
    precision.
I never see the colony as more than an organic machine.

Now we are near the end. The inner voice murmurs *perhaps you went
    too far.*
Outside we still crave the sense of a mysterious world
reaching endlessly beyond us. And how can we find it?

E. O. Wilson is frustrating and beguiling at once, as he writes so
evocatively and poetically for a scientist, showing how art and science might be combined to provide a fuller view of knowing nature.
In his recent book *Consilience* he states, "The love of complexity
without reductionism makes art; the love of complexity with reductionism makes science." Unfortunately, he wants science to encompass, contain, and explain art as merely one small domain within
itself, rather than considering them as parallel, intertwining ways
of reaching the world. I massaged his earlier words above to bring
out an inherent ambiguity that he tends to pretend isn't there.

Wilson really thinks nature can be understood as an "organic machine." I believe, however, that the mechanical and the living always
act in tension with each other. When we explain things, we brush
over the most radical truths. Art must grab us instantly, before we

know what hit us. Art offers real knowledge that reverberates inside ourselves like the memories of perfect-sounding waves, it presents sudden truths that do not profit from reduction to principles or rules. Sure, science advances, and as it does more and more information comes into our reach; but explanation is still only one of many ways of knowing and perceiving.

Fitting into the world, searching for a sense of place, will always require art in addition to information. So I advise you to listen to the world not for data, but for presence. And do not listen not just to locate yourself in space, but to enjoy what you hear. What you hear will be a world more alive than annoying, more beautiful than distracting. Wake up to birds and not to alarm clocks, fall asleep when noises part the airwaves into silence.

Does listening make one a better person? I hear that from my friends. "Now I understand why I had no friends at college!" says one. "I didn't know how to listen. I've worked hard at *listening* lately," he adds, having taken a cue from self-help books. Bravo, I say. But listen to the whole world, not just to what people say. Sounds should enhance us, not diminish us.

Sound in film, television, and on radio continues to be mediated, in an attempt to approach abstract ideas of perfection. It's amazing what can be tweaked, fine-tuned, fixed. Working on a film project recently, I heard the words of one voice being blended with the inflection of another! It's hard to tell who or what you're hearing these days. With all the ability we now have to mix and match, reshuffle and reverberate sound, we may need to learn greater powers of listening and discrimination.

As you attend to sound, you will come to hear everything around as something that can be manipulated, even the most natural and enfolding of noises. How is it made? What are it rules? All sounds become tools or the result of tools, dug, hammered, cut, molded out of any raw materials we can imagine.

But we don't want to go that far. Remember the sense of peace that comes from fitting in to the sounds of the place you are. They open you up, rather than tying you down. Approach that reverberant ecstasy that comes from before, you and your shadow united with single tones and moments encompassing all that is and all that could be. There is a world of sound, true, but it is our world. We don't automatically fit in to it, we have to work to fit in, to roam and listen. A world of many human musics also invites us to listen and to learn.

FOUR-FIFTHS OF THE WORLD

CANNOT BE WRONG

The world becomes ever smaller the more we learn about it. With the multitudes that now live on Earth, its far reaches now appear all the closer. We have endless images of the exotic in our heads, whether from films, from television, from the Internet. Nowhere is too remote to have some sense of today. The same goes for the world's music, which today is accessible on glimmering silver disks: digital laser technology reducing sounds to bytes, a computer recombining and resuscitating it. Add an electronic danceable beat, and you have the homogenizing club music of the future.

We're talking about music as *product* here, and fast forget its power to move masses, to inspire those in its throes toward ecstasy and trance. Ah, what difference does it make, the music made among us or blaring from huge speakers front and back? The more tremendous, the more universal music is, the more it binds us all together. All the world enjoys music, and there is a certain sameness in popular music that allows it to be sold and loved with a frenzy everywhere. On the other hand, there is a shadow music, sounds that come out of alleys and canyons, from single drums and one-string guitars and flutes without holes, and this basic primal sound has its roots everywhere. The world market for a mass culture may suppress it, but it is still there, you can hear it, you can even buy it wherever records are sold because, after all, nearly everything is for sale these days.

You can buy it, but that might not make you live it. You can listen to it, you might play it back and study it, but that won't necessarily make the music essential. Music may be universal, but it is not a language to be understood; it is more of a yearning—to move, to sing, to express, to change the world as we live in it. If the music *ever* goes just as we expect it to, then we are consuming it, not participating in its creation. As much as the market wants music to become a thing that is bought and sold, its power lies elsewhere.

The listening to nature I described in the previous chapter can be done anywhere, as it is mainly about being sensitive to where you are, not about seeking the untrammeled and pure. If you listen closely to your surroundings, you will discover the music of the place, sounds that resonate with your location, your country, your culture. The evidence suggests the possibility of common values that encompass the globe; after all, isn't that something we all want?

Consensus respect for human rights, nature's rights, freedom of spirit, and a wish to let differences coexist? If so in ethics, why not in art? In the realm of art, we feel that a loss of diversity would be sad and unacceptable.

Music stores today have a section that wasn't there a generation ago: "world music." But isn't all music world music, since we're all in this world, and all music comes from here? Let's think of world music instead as music of place, art that celebrates where it comes from. It doesn't need to mark its difference by announcing it, by singing in strange languages or employing exotic sound effects. Nevertheless, it tends to be based on qualities somewhat different from what we're used to in Western history. The epigram to the encyclopedia *The Rough Guide to World Music* says it best. The words are those of Hijaz Mustapha, of the pseudo–Middle Eastern pop band 3 Mustaphas 3 (actually four white guys from London): "Four-fifths of the world cannot be wrong." What does this mean? I think I know: Most of the world's music is not based on harmonic movement, or on songs with AABA forms. Rather, it's based on the use of a single tonality throughout an entire piece and, more important, on a driving rhythm—the *groove*—that never lets up, be it slow or fast, seductive or danceable, easy or relentless.

World music sounds exotic because it frequently seems to have no beginning or end, and it is often based on cascades of uncountable rhythms that emerge from a group fervor rather than from individuals following paperbound rules. There are not even measures to count, no four-four beats to latch on to. Just a moving swirl. You know, that's one of my favorite words for it: *swirl.* The swirl may be hard, even impossible, to pinpoint, but it grabs us all the same. For we are still part of the world, despite the peculiarity of our culture. We still know about the groove.

It's that rhythm, that pulse that seems regular but just a bit off, that you want to dance to. Swing, get that feel, that edge. Polyrhythms—4 against 3, 5 against 8—not as a calculated exercise, but as a natural urge to merge and to blend. Although machines driving the popular techno pulse can emulate the groove, it's only when the beat goes a little bit askew, becomes just a tad unpredictable, that we are really drawn into it. The one-fifth of the world that is ours has promoted an art music that backs off from rhythm, a music that uses rhythm as a device but doesn't *submit* to it. It has never denied that the pulse exists, but it has always considered it to be a bit common or vulgar, and has therefore attenuated it in the service of "higher" rules of harmony and delicacy. Sure, there is a point to refinement, but in the process something natural or gritty or dirty or dangerous is trampled down or pushed aside.

The key to understanding the pulse of the planet is to give in to that rhythmic power, yet still be able to jump from one culture to another, joining in with whatever you have to offer. That should be the education of the musician: to learn how to join in in unfamiliar musical situations, to improvise when you don't know the rules. Not to be the star and sing out above the fray, but to slip in; to go native; to figure out quickly what others like and what they dislike.

We can always use new ways of assembling rhythm. We can always search for new beats that will make us want to stand up and move. It's tempting to take even the strangest of musics and transform them into ours: For pop music, make the syncopations and polyrhythms into an electronic, perfectly regular beat. For classical, transform the intonation to equal temperament and add the planned discipline of the written score. In jazz, make the drone instrument a wailing saxophone and substitute familiar instruments for exotic ones.

But no, don't do it that way. Do the opposite. Learn the foreign rules. Make something that may at first sound strange indeed, but that taps into the primal forces that lure us into the world's music in the first place. I do not want to like something solely because it is different, exotic. I want to be honestly open to the search for an organic otherness that lies latent inside me. The world should never be boring. Indeed, we should be looking far across it for new sources of energy and drive. Then let them work upon us before we subsume them into our usual ways.

The groove. The pulse that cannot be tracked or named. Once in it, you don't want it to end. It must be a fact of life that leads you on into a solid place in the world of things. Why did human beings learn to mark time? Not just to place an order on the days, but so they could dance, so they could feel a rhythm out there that is larger than us, a journey complete enough not to need departure or destination.

Much has been written about the music of different parts of the world, what makes each territory's melodies and sounds different from all others. Less has been said about the worldliness of the world's grooves, however, this quality that holds so many of the world's musics together but that remains outside our own, outside what we have been taught to obey. A few films succeed in getting us inside these grooves. Tony Gatlif's wonderful *Latcho Drom* (Safe Journey, 1993) is a remarkable film consisting entirely of scenes of live performances by Gypsy musicians. Part ethnographic document, part poetic picture, part pungent rhapsody, the film portrays the movement of this quintessentially wandering people across the continents and cultures of our world, beginning in India, ending in Spain. There is no narration, virtually no dialog, and subtitles appear only sporadically, translating lyrics that are passionate and strange, like the music itself.

The music in this film seems to describe a culture that borrows from genres wherever it goes, part of the fierce drive to live, prosper, and move on from each place that it reaches. "I curse the astrologer," sings a boy on the way to a wedding, "for telling me to marry someone so far from my family and my home. I'm going to burn my horoscope." The procession advances on, accompanied by the rhythm of the jingling caravan. At the ceremony, the men sit on one side, the women on the other. The groom begins a soliloquy that lures those gathered into song: "I have prepared foods, and fruits from many lands . . . for you. I have laid my bed in a delicious spot. It is empty . . . without you." And the *ghatam* drums kick in, the band is clapping and driving the dance onward, the *ghazal*-like singing soars up and around the beat, reminiscent of other Indian vocal music, but less refined, more extreme. The seeds of flamenco emotion are already here.

Sitarist Amit Chatterjee remarked to me that the farther the Gypsies spread from India, the less happy they are. And the film reveals that, as does the soundtrack, though it contains less information. Egypt; Turkey. On to Romania, for a fabulous song of pathos where an old toothless violinist, accompanied by a cembalom, sings about the fall of an empire: "Ceausescu the criminal . . . he has destroyed this country. Bucuresti, Timosoara, what are the people doing? They are shooting at people—this is it, it's all over for the tyrant. Nicolai has destroyed Romania, there is nothing left." And he's playing his violin by unraveling the string, dismantling his instrument, just as his country has been unhinged by the tragic course of history.

But next, an incredible pyrotechnic dance of crazy rhythms and questionable intonation, an amazing attempt at unison virtuosity. This is how it is with Gypsy music, as it swings viciously from the joyous to the despairing and back. In a people's music is their strength, and this sound is strong medicine indeed. By the time they track through Germany and France, finally to reach Spain, the tone is angry, vengeful, tough, a cry shaken at the wealthy in their white houses at the edge of town: "Sometimes I even envy the way you treat your dog." Music saves them, keeps the wanderers smiling.

And although they've learned from the cultures they pass through, much more borrowing than stealing, their music is definitely their own, marked by their own cultural sadness.

The Gypsies have suffered, been misunderstood, made an effort *not* to fit in wherever they go. They were happier at the start of their journey. If there is to be a return, it will only be back to an unfamiliar place that welcomes them without knowing them. Since the film's release the world has embraced these musicians, giving thunderous ovations at concerts, but forgetting the centuries-long oppression of the people and their music.

Why film as a vehicle for world music? The answer is simple: It is the most total way to gain familiarity with distant worlds that are concurrent with our own. Surrounding and gripping the senses, film is more powerful than video (though video, to be sure, is more accessible). Image cannot replace reality, but it does augment reality. We soon feel what it is like to be a Gypsy on the move, banished from home, moving westward toward our own suspicious world. Rhythm remains the way to win us over.

Another film, *Lucky People Center International* (1998), exploits this global power of the pulse in a completely different way. The film is a Swedish project, made by the performance collective Lucky People Center. Originally from Gothenburg, now based in Stockholm, they were once a jazz big band, then evolved into a techno/rave happening kind of group, mixing visual imagery with songs cut and pasted from provocative news pieces. It's constructed digital music. When played live, machines provide the beats, but they are interesting, driving beats, and the whole audience moves and gets caught in the surge. What separates this endeavor from so many other attempts to mix found material with live jamming is its favoring of optimism and hope over irony. Brian Eno and David Byrne did something similar twenty years ago with *My Life in the*

Bush of Ghosts, but the words were incomplete, dark. Here there is more joy.

For their *International* film project, the group traveled far and wide across the globe filming rhythms, energies, and the spiritual practices of people who embrace strong beliefs, strong passions. Voudou ceremonies. Capoeira in Brazil. The struggle of the Penan in Malaysia against the government and foreign industry's devastation of their forest homes. A Tokyo banker who plays nightly in a loud, noise-music ensemble to vent his rage against the machine in the midst of machines. Annie Sprinkle speaking the gospel of pleasure of the self. A scientist who studies the origins of music in primates with the calls of the gibbon in the tropical forest, and extrapolates toward humanity. "Man . . . must dance." A contorted swami meditating upside down; he checks his watch, it's time, he unravels himself and resumes his feet. "Seek, seek," says Baba Ghi. "You must keep asking questions." The film clip, repeated, is mixed with an electronic, but living, pulse. The action on the screen turns into something like a music video, an image framed by the incessant beat. A Maori war dance band, Te Waka Huia, is singing what is apparently an old song, with the drums beating and the men chanting in unison. But what are they saying? We outsiders have to read the subtitles: "A monster is coming. It is called the year 2000. All our children will need credit cards. They will need money to pay for these cards in the year 2000. Everything is changing." The old is the new, the ancient ways live on and confront the present. But we all must dance.

It's difficult to describe this film in words, though it is somewhat in the tradition of the better-known image/music mixes *Koyaanisqatsi* and *Baraka*. The difference here is a willingness to let the world's rhythms speak for themselves, rather than to impose an element of bombast. It's often easier to use our own rhythms than to listen to what's out there. To learn from the world's musics, however, we have to be genuinely open to the unfamiliar, willing to relinquish a sense of control, though an organizing idea to make sense of all the confusion is necessary as well. *Latcho Drom* used the Gypsies' westward-moving exile to explore a force that moves through the world's musics, as these migrants learn from other cultures, and even change them, even while remaining something to be chased from the nations of landed peoples, eternally homeless. *Lucky People,* for its part, takes arresting stories and images from many different cultures and glues them together with a common pulse that meets all our needs. The Lucky People collective is not afraid of the new, the unsteady, or the machine. It wants to convince us, by massaging the hard edge through the mix of soft possibility.

Then there are stories that make the leap between one musical culture and another. Blind San Francisco bluesman Paul Pena is sitting at home in the early nineties, depressed after the death of his wife. He spends the days listening to shortwave radio stations, hearing the far-off limits of the world. He tunes into something that sounds like distortion on the airwaves, sliding harmonics venturing in and out of phase. Pretty soon he realizes it's a strange kind of singing, from a place he's never heard of, the tiny country of Tuva, just north of Mongolia, once in the Soviet Union, now a Russian republic. Pena goes around the corner to his local record store, gets hold of a Smithsonian Folkways disk featuring Tuvan throat-singing, and starts to learn this special technique, by which one shapes the mouth's cavity to control the character of overtones produced by the voice, enabling two and sometimes three notes to come out. From the natural harmonic series come the same root resonances that make all music possible. The Tuvans have stayed with such resonances rather than dividing and conquering them into so many transposable scales, thus taking the opposite tack from Western music. This far-off place and its music have fascinated other explorers, from religion scholar Huston Smith in the mid-1960s to Richard Feynman, who as a far-out physicist and bongo player got obsessed with the place in his final years but sadly died in 1988, just before he was finally granted permission to visit the capital of Kyzyl, with its Bactrian camels and wrestling rings. Over there, every little kid can throat sing; it's just something people learn to do.

By the time Pena met Kongar-ool Ondar in the early nineties, Tuvan music was becoming a pop-exotica phenomenon. Ondar's group, Huun Huur Tu, was touring the world to standing ovations. Snippets of the technique were heard on all sorts of records, as pop music is always looking for an outlandish blast to dress up the familiar. What does it take, though, for the exotic to be more than a fleeting effect, more than a curiosity in a field where there is already too much to hear, too much to choose from? The answer comes when someone delves deeper into it, makes it essential to their being, sustains them on the inside. In 1994 Pena approached Ondar after a sold-out show in San Francisco and sang him a Tuvan song. Immediately the singer said, "You must come to our grand competition next year and sing there."

The film *Genghis Blues,* by Roko and Adrian Belic, describes Pena's journey to the distant land of overtones in a rough-cut but careful style. With Pena on this unlikely expedition is a motley crew of hippie backup musicians as well as venerable Los Angeles world music DJ Mario Casetta, frail but determined. In the end, Pena is nothing less than a sensation. Although Feynman may have brought Tuva international recognition, he never went there as a contender. Pena won the competition (in a new category created just for him), and in the process taught the locals a thing or two about the blues.

The upper pitches of the harmonic series, as I've said before, are in between the piano's keynotes, but they're right on when it comes to the blues. We crave those in-between spaces because they are natural, primary. We hear them right down to the gut, from Kyzyl to San Francisco.

Tuvan music has lasted for thousands of years and transcends the peculiarities of culture and custom. It is universally graspable, though by nothing so exact as a word or a rule. It is *this* universe that world music guides us onto, and it is this part of music that jumps easily from one way of life to the next. Though not the mainstream of what is offered to us in the marketplace of sound, it can be found there, even in the least likely of places.

I mention these three films because they make the reality of this other way a little bit more clear.

We already know what the blues and Tuva have in common. Not the chords, not just the feel, but the resonances down through the bones. What about scales, notes? Why is Irish music popular all over the world, such that even African music is now blending in its elements? The pentatonic scale, five open notes, dancing up and down through pennywhistles and pipes—this sound is everywhere. Found in many cultures, it ties us all together. At the same time, it needs the bends, the ornamentation, the pathos of people's specific suffering, the joyful lilts and trills, to expand upon it and to tie it down to a place, somewhere real in the world.

In the future, will African and Irish music sound the same?

You might consider this experimentation as the latest round of colonialism. The ethnomusicologist Steven Feld, who brought the ecomusical ideas of "lift-up-over sounding" to us from the Bosavi people of New Guinea, has also delved into the various ways pygmy music has been co-opted by pop music, from Herbie Hancock's "Watermelon Man" to Deep Forest. Actually, he tells us, even the ancient Egyptians used the pygmy techniques of hocketing back and forth between words, flutes, and breath over bottles. Still, says Feld, it's not right to take a piece of the exotic and cash in on it. Instead he speaks favorably of the approach taken by the Belgian group Zap Mama, several singers, some African, some European, who learn the songs in their original languages and adapt them with new arrangements, creating a globally fused choral sound.

There are tales from all over that suggest how much more music can mean if it connects us to nature, if it drives us deep inside to our roots, if it dances us together with other animals, with plants, with rocks and water, with the *rest* of the world. Four-fifths, nine-tenths, twenty-seven–twenty-ninths, one small part of the billions of possibilities beyond the human sphere: we have so much to learn, and that's what keeps us going, not the demonstrated evidence of progress but the sense of there always being more to take in, to learn from, to offer a hand in the dance.

Think of the Micmac legend about the woman who can't sit still, who has to dance on, deep down, far beneath the surface of the earth. "She dances faster and faster. The dance is filling her with something; she has the Power in her. Power is filling her, and as it does, one of those oysters begins to change its shape. . . . This oyster is shaping itself into a whale. The old woman's dance is calling it." Getting deep into the groove of things, going far beyond human form. Many cultures have stories about the devil's irresistible violin playing, or about an instrument that sucks people up in its potential for virtuosity. "Why," they say up in the Maine woods, "the mosquitoes are thicker than fiddlers in hell!" There is something dangerous about the grooves that capture the soul. They pull us in, and there is no escape. The drums that do not stop, or the hypnotizing scales, five notes, four, not much more. A few notes; a few universal notes. We've heard them for centuries, and they'll still be around long after all shards of civilization have turned to dust. It's close to the natural spread of tones, the wind in the trees and the waves crashing on rock. Listen to it all, find a way to join in that doesn't dissolve it. That's how to play with the rhythms of the world, to earn yourself a place in nature.

This mania for fitting into the larger world, from where does it come? Maybe once it was underlain by an environmental responsibility, the desire to do something right for the earth. With that, today, comes a kind of guilt, with the realization that until now we have done so much wrong. But at the same time, surely we did something right? Or is our one-fifth hopelessly doomed to be ambitious, earth-transforming, ignorant, and far removed from the natural grooves. This easy remorse is reminiscent of original sin, suggested by all the old religions. Think of it instead as a puzzle, something we can work at: Let us do good as we strive to understand. Let us inhabit paradox and not just brush it away. It is hard for the powerful culture to learn from others when all that bolsters us is so destructive. The diverse native ways never had a chance against all our guns, germs, and steel, as Jared Diamond has so aptly argued. But what of their music? Can we learn from it without co-opting it? But neither do we want to preserve it as in a museum. Instead we must make it part of the future culture of the world, a better culture than today's, one with more diversity, more life, more nature, more song.

Look at the real world, though: there's a cheesy electro soundtrack blaring from the same Asian loudspeakers that carry the muezzins' morning prayers. That fabulous, pure, polyrhythmic Bulgarian folk music survived in part with the assistance of state terror, and in China Maoist pronouncements ensured that music would be of the people, of the folk, not taking on the decadent influences of the capitalist West. Now as we *all* become the capitalist West, differences will blur, and all will want the same stars, symbols of Hollywood prosperity, illusive glitter and wealth.

The world loses its mystery, its rareness, in all this global access to sound and light. Nothing is truly unfamiliar anymore. Anything goes. Yet that doesn't mean that all places will serve up the same soundtracks, with everyone marching to an enforced beat from above. That's how people describe it when they don't want to like it. But how different is that from everybody grooving to a beat from below? The pulse of the earth, the pulse of the people, the rhythm that dances us deep under the ground? See, music is so open, so malleable, so far from logic and language that we can make it mean whatever we want. Better perhaps to clap, chant, sing, play, and "move any way you like, that's what we do," as some Nepali kids told me years ago, playing Michael Jackson on the Himalayan village's one and only boom box while they watched the strange white people dance.

The music pounding on from the rest of the world does not need to begin or end. Its structure provides the beat, the grounding force, announcing that it has always been here and always will be. At work could be the rhythmic pattern, could be the drone note, could be the presence of the ancient rules. An Indian raga, for example, is not quite a scale, not quite a melody, not quite the same up as down, not quite the improvisation within it versus being lost outside. These structures, delicate and hard to master, are *always there;* they are places you may choose to play in or listen to for a while, but then, when you fall back outside them to reality, the music remains. Even while we're not there, the music rages on. It's inside us, it's written down in the rules of the culture, it's part of some common, lasting thread. It is the art that has no beginning or end, far removed from Aristotle's carefully detailed structure of how things start and how they finish. This is the rest of the world, *muchachos,* and we are in it.

How we stay in it is a matter of choice. Lamont Young's got a drone piece going that must continue aumming for a thousand years or the world will fall apart. We celebrate composers who proffer unique kinds of instruction, not those who keep a tradition alive and unsigned. Sure, we have our exacting and meticulous rules as well, but we can see culture advancing even as rules are broken. Might all this individuality only be a phase?

Of course, I too want to be different. But I want to make something necessary, essential, eternal. Whatever I make will be thus simple, not too much in itself, some bridge from my individual world to the general force the world needs now. I feel not part of any tradition nearby, but neither am I drawn to faraway traditions, only to specific pieces within them: those, especially, that seem to have no beginning and no end.

On the clarinet I find myself searching for repeatable patterns of notes, patterns not familiar but never heard before; I look for such groupings to play again and again, not just as exercises, but to make them essential to my music. (Perhaps this is how Philip Glass developed his penchant for the mechanical.) I want to make sure each repetition sounds different from the last, and from the next, so that the variation that makes the natural world possible also finds its way into my music. Italo Calvino's Mr. Palomar stared at the brink of the ocean and was unable to isolate one wave from any other, so quickly did they roll and fall over each other into a surf of imponderable but still-present rhythm. We want beat and recurrence to be like that, building intensity but hard to figure out. Resisting analysis. There is a Finnish folksong with a rhythmic pattern 5 6 5 6 6 7 5 7, which seems very weird to most Western ears; but when you hear the song you realize at once that it *works* and wonder if the whole impulse to count it out might be missing the point, missing the gentle flow of beat after extra beat after missing beat that makes this a song that can still be danced to, indeed, *must* be danced to to make sense of it. Music is not out there to keep us still.

We can learn grooves from all over the world and adapt them to our purposes, but often the result is mush. Music ends up slipping into the realm of the familiar whether we want it to or not—since listeners (or consumers, anyway) want to know what they're getting. The problem here is that world music is usually sorted by country, which means trouble for any musician who blends African poly-rhythms with Celtic optimism, or Zen pathos with Islamic fervor. North and south find no place at all when they become lost inside each other's borders.

Real world music cannot be saved by identity politics. It doesn't exist to represent any particular ethnic group, country, or part of the world. I'm told that the music I play should be called "world music," no longer jazz. Yet it is from the jazz tradition that I have learned to praise individuality in performance. In jazz, the unique-ness of improvised soloing comes first. It's a form of egotism, but it does ally me to this one genre of music. One person makes the music, out of materials collected and assumed. In jazz, the playing must be more distinctive than the composition, the situation, or the rules.

I take this from jazz, and I try to maintain it in all the music I do, even when it grates against the dictates of other styles. As Stravinsky once said, "The more constraints I place upon myself, the greater creativity is possible." Still, the odds are stacked against pieces that combine many genres, for the criteria by which to judge them are so unclear. They can always defend themselves by hiding behind the claim of difference ("This isn't *that* kind of music, don't expect it to be anything like what you already know"). But without aesthetic guidelines—without discussion of what makes one work succeed and another fail—there can be no good or bad in art. And without objective means of establishing good and bad, we cannot be free from likes and dislikes, only from care and from quality. In that case, we will have to rely on the market or convention to decide.

(This may be the philosopher in me talking, the nay-saying beast, the skeptical inquirer, but not someone who refuses to believe in the value of things that cannot be explained. I never want to explain away art when I question its quality, I only want people—the makers, the takers, the buyers, the sellers—to transcend personal preference and try to make ours a civilization of quality, one that cares about bringing beauty into our lives and will not rest until it is there and we know it and want it and will keep it coming, ever in new and more dynamic ways.)

Much world music lapses into the expected bankable grooves of monocultural pop, or the easy calm of a technologically enforced new-age aesthetic of relaxation. Neither approach asks for surprises—at least not too many surprises. Too much art pleases us enough to keep us complacent, or else screams as an affront to our complacency. Not enough offers a navigable way from the expected into the forest of the new.

The best example of a figure who used the music of the world to bolster his own jazz expression would have to be trumpeter Don Cherry, who came out of the raucous, R&B-based experimental exuberance of the Ornette Coleman band at the end of the 1950s. Here was a musician with quirky technique, but who took supreme joy in every note he let loose. There is in his playing such love and surprise, such groove and discovery, such a presence of the individual man as he follows the beats and breaks the rules, carefully but suddenly escaping the expected and the clear. When Cherry hit a wrong note, he would not let his playing apologize. Instead he would use the mistake, explore it, show us how hard it is to know wrong note from right if you've got that feel.

When he began to travel the world and pick up new tricks—

whistle-flutes from India, *dousongoni* guitars from Mali, assorted Indonesian bells and gongs—Cherry didn't relegate it all to ornamental exotica. Rather, he used it, added it to his artful expressiveness. In so doing, he adopted the same openness to accident, inserting his personal voice into all kinds of musical contexts. If you listen to his work in which he consciously tries to blend the influences of many cultures, it may at first seem easy to figure out or to imitate. Why is it, then, that so many replications of his approach lack his luster and immediacy? I think it is because they lack the emotional availability of good jazz soloing. A solo must be based on love; it must be played outward, to the audience; it must also reach from the past to the future, coming from somewhere, even if it's somewhere undefinable, unidentifiable, and pushing the music forward. The music is jazz if this soloing, this individual and sudden invention of the melody, is still the core of what's going on, what people want to hear, what the musicians want to play. The ego doesn't drive it; rather, it comes from an urge to create a living whole from different sounds, something that is constantly changing, moving, with a life of its own but also a place somewhere in the master plan. Although it is a challenge, the goal can be to make something that helps humanity *fit in to nature*. This may be easy for other life forms, but it is hard for us, caught as we are in our own arbitrary rules that simplify the world beyond belief: rectangles; four-four time; beginnings, middles, and ends. The world out there admits none of this. It is a booming, buzzing confusion, and will stay that way long after we give up trying to reduce it to principles and laws.

Don Cherry brought life into every single note he played. Each tone showed a way into the wholeness. It's hard to talk about it, even harder to do. Music is so malleable that it is possible to say almost *anything* about it, to massage our perceptions however we want. That is why it exists, I suppose, why it will never be subsumed or replaced by words. The description of the music should not, after all, be more interesting than the music itself. That's called advertising, or the public relations of art. The words, rather, should lead us in, cause us to really listen and, finally, to reconsider sounds we may previously have taken for granted, sounds that before we listened meant nothing to us, that were only part of the world.

There is sound, there is chaos, there is anarchy, and yet there is a plan behind it all. Can this approach I write of be applied over the entire world? I took a trip to India once to play some music, a trip into the fervent pulse of foreign sounds. I went to make some bridge music in the service of the wild, to see whether some of this between-music might have something to contribute to the environmental cause. Here's a record of that journey:

I'm here to play some music, at a gathering of hundreds of people committed to saving the wild places of this earth. The Sixth World Wilderness Congress, the first such meeting to be held in Asia. Wild places mean something very different in a populous Asian country than they mean in the United States, where we set aside lands that are largely devoid of human activity. Here people proliferate, and they live together with the animals in a crazy kind of beauty.

Silence is hard to come by in India, no one has much personal space. But the buzz of activity is so wonderful, so complete, so human, that the idea of alienation and loneliness seems to be little more than a possible fiction. Listen; listen to the chaos, and dream of the order. How can such a busy country produce a music so precise and so eternal? How does the perfection and order of Indian improvisations connect to the grand mix of humanity that makes up this territory? This is what I'm here to find out.

A drive from the airport down crazy streets instantly brought back a euphoria I had almost forgotten. The first rush was not one of poverty, sickness, crowding, or confusion, but of sheer joy. So much was happening, so many people, so much movement. Here, I thought while we snaked through traffic in the big rounded car, it would be impossible to be bored. Not only the colors, sounds, and smells but also the language are so vibrant. This must be the home of at least half the English speakers on Earth.

A huge billboard in the center of town towers red above the rustling black smoke, asking a Hindu koan: "Is Bill Clinton really remorseful?" Nearby, in front of the grand, sprawling parliament houses of the state of Karnataka, was a message neither Republican nor Democrat would erect even in my own rather fundamentalist country: "The Government! Doing God's Work—Here on Earth." Think what you want on the perils or promise of globalization, you can't help but be swept up by the rich mélange of creative excitement, by the way ideas and practices seem to spread before our eyes. "Xanadu Village: The Clubhouse of the Future" is under construction just past the city limits. Stop for lunch at the "Energy Kebab Centre," and finish off with Krishna Koffee, which we are assured is "a 100% blend of modernity and tradition."

Modern or traditional: where do you draw the line? That is what I'm here to find out, the truth of a world as ancient as history and still evolving toward a future way. Yes! Yes! One hundred percent of the past and the future. I'm there! I'm there! A resort an hour outside the capital offers everything I'll need: "Food! Stay! Nature!"

That, too, is what I had come for. To create music, in honor of the World Wilderness Congress, that was faithful to a vision of a live and natural earth, and to find a way to combine my own Western music with the Indian music of the place into an international whole. That is the task at hand, but so far all that grabs me are not sounds but images, not even traditional images, but images of the clash: the splendor of the past and the seductions of the present; the grounded world here and the dreams of faraway come near. The one hundred percent blend—I am fully inside it.

In a sense, Indian and Western music have absolutely nothing to do with one another. Theirs is based on the ever-presence of rhythm and a single grounding tone, with melody being the prevailing force that pulls improvisations out of the hearts and fingers of trained players who have worked for many years to play freely amid the exacting slew of rules. Ours, in contrast, places harmony and form first, and moves exacting colors and timbres from one tonal center to another, around and around, only sometimes to end up back where we began. It is said that a great connoisseur of Indian classical music once bolted from the front row of Carnegie Hall at the moment the music modulated from one key to another—he couldn't believe a piece of music could be so undisciplined!

In our culture, we expect that movement, and are often bored by the drone of Asian music, ho-hummed by its tenacity, by the fact that it won't ever shut up and go away. At least, we're supposed to be bored. Me, I never cared much for chords and changes, for beginnings, middles, and ends. I've always wanted my music simply to *exist,* to flow, to sound as if it has always been here, something we can tune into for a while, then tune out of, while it, singing on, remains.

So I'm not the best person to invite for such an "East/West Fusion" event, since I'd been adrift in musical exile for years, divorced from any discipline that would try to have me. Fitting in nowhere in particular, I am understandably nervous when I go for my first meeting with the esteemed singer R. A. Ramamani and her accompanying band, the Karnataka College of Percussion, led by her husband, T. A. S. Mani.

This thunderous ensemble is known the world over for their energetic approach to traditional south Indian music, as well as their willingness to collaborate with various western artists, notably the jazz saxophonists Charlie Mariano and Iain Bellamy, the percussionist Tunji Beier, and Egyptian nay master Mohammed El Toukhi. I was honored to be invited to join them for this event to celebrate the promise of wilderness in India and the rest of the developing but still wild world.

After a short nap to unjetlag myself following the eighteen-hour flight from New York, I take an auto rickshaw through the bustle to the other side of town. Here the streets offer a comfortable atmosphere simply by being at a human scale. A house is being constructed brick by brick across the street from the building where I am to meet the band. A few donkeys are standing in the street down the block to the left, and cars are maneuvering around them. A fortune teller advertises "correct predictions" with a rusting giant hand sign emblazoned with the strange curlicued Kannada script. A coconut merchant slowly wheels his cart, wielding a sharp machete; ask for one and the blade comes down: water to slake your thirst.

Inside the house the band is waiting for me, smiling, sitting on the floor, each next to a kind of drum that I have not seen before. The *mridangam* is basic, the lead drum in south Indian music, like the more familiar north Indian tabla but compressed into one, with two tuned heads, high and low, each marked by a large black spot around which you control the tone and the pitch. Then there is the bigger *tavil,* a two-headed bass drum, and the clay-pot *ghatam,* my favorite, with its *whoom whoom baoop baoop* range of gulping sounds. A small tambourine called a *kanjira,* made from the stretched skin of a monitor lizard, is played with the fingers of a hand that must be constantly dipped into water to keep the tone liquid and fresh. And finally there is a Jew's harp (*boing boing*) called the *morsing.*

South Indian music is quite different from the familiar north Indian music of sitar, tabla, and drone. This music is driven by the beat—not a single *tala* that remains unchanged throughout the piece, but rhythms that respond and react to the melodies, speeding up, slowing down, keeping all together, a primal, heartbeat force. The heavy drums sound east African at times, suggesting the famed Burundi beat that the pop group Adam and the Ants co-opted in the early 1980s.

Listening to the tapes from my time there, I find the rehearsals sound much better than the final concert. They are looser, full of the flavor of the place, with street noises mixing together with shouts and *konakkol* drum language, in which the musicians "talk" through the rhythms at lightning speed. There is also a frenzy of discussion, which to the outsider who doesn't understand the words becomes an extra layer of music. Energy, verve, push, the buzz—call it what you will, it was an exciting mess to be in the midst of.

There was more experimentation in the practice sessions. By the time we hit the concert, it had been worked out and the music was more subdued. At least on their part. Me, I was hunting for my way all along. Listening back, I like to hear that freshness, the search for musical possibility. That's what improvisation is about, and Indian musicians have the most sophisticated understanding of improvisation on the planet. There are rules for how to move up the scale, and other rules for how to move back down. The melody drives the motion, rather than the harmony governing the melody, as we are used to in the West.

"Play as you like, improvise as you like. Do not worry too much about our rules. Use your rules," Mr. Mani told me, wanting me to feel at ease. The strange thing was, I felt more at ease with this music than with what was supposed to be my own. I do not know why this was so.

What could this cross-cultural music have to do with wilderness? The answer hangs on the very idea of wilderness, and the way it intersects with human cultures.

Every one of the world's languages probably has a word for *wild*. Uncontrollable passions and forces, energies that follow no order and buck civilization at its edges, or even right in its midst. In some tongues *wilderness* means the same as wasteland; in our own sacred texts it once meant the empty, uninhabitable deserts where our heroes' faith was tested. Only with the spread and success of organized and material culture has the wild become something that needs to be saved. We feel ourselves stronger, more in control, and we venture to protect what once was feared.

The only thing is, this wilderness that has so captivated the American consciousness is clear only because we, who define ourselves in terms of our frontier push always to expand, can imagine it is an empty place. First treacherous, it is now precious as it loses its true and pure state.

India does not have that innocence. It is an ancient country, and even the homes of tigers and leopards are places where people have lived for centuries. The American model of people out, animals in, seems naive here, as it does for much of the developing world. Yet human populations are increasing, and many wild animals are in danger. These World Wilderness gatherings, which are held every four years in different parts of the world, are therefore convened to explore whether a sense of respect for the wild can make sense even in a place with so different a history as this.

The traditional music of India has an inherent wildness that also contains exactness. As it is improvised, it is spontaneous and unexpected; like jazz, it is created as it spins itself out. It is philosophical music, because the musicians are thinking out loud, testing as they go. Unlike jazz, however, it has precise rules that cannot be bent. Wrong notes cannot become right notes. I feel an affinity for the Indian approach. I don't like it when the key changes, when the music modulates away from its essential center. Why not stay in one place, where there is so much to explore?

The music is worthy of wilderness when it can sound both safe and dangerous at once.

The concert comes at the end of a long day of speeches and salutations. The delegates are worn out, but the hall is almost full. Ramamani had asked for eleven microphones, and now that the band is setting up I can see why. Our group is bigger than any of the incarnations I had rehearsed with, including now a violinist, a few extra drummers, and one guy who recites the language of the drums. Everyone is close-miked to keep their individuality as they are blended by an expert soundman. Behind the group a huge green banner reads: "6th World Wilderness Congress, Bangalore, India: The Call for a Sustainable Future."

What is it we are to sustain? The wild places of the planet, for sure. But also the beat, the drone tone, and the melody. First the Karnataka College plays, featuring vocal improvisation over the thundering drums. Then I do a set of solo clarinet over a taped background of natural sounds and electronic rhythms, aided by R. A. Rajagopalan on the ghatam. Then we play several pieces together, and I try not to compete with diva Ramamani, but to complement her as best as I can. Still, rules are made to be broken. Why not solo at the same time, mix one invented melody with another, so as to confuse the egos? Music is not like a conversation—why not have more voices going on at the same time? And why not break out of the official notes of the raga scale, bend toward both the familiar and the unfamiliar?

I don't know what result I'm going for, only that I want it to be more wild, more unpredictable, less like the many fusions of Indian music and jazz that I had heard before.

After the show, a smooth, mustached character comes up to me and invites me to play with some local rock musicians the next night at an outdoor amphitheater in the city. "It's a mixed crowd, you can never tell who will show up, but I think you ought to come down and show those people some *music*. Bend their ears a little."

The next day he picks me up at the hotel and we take an auto-rickshaw to another side of town. We enter a dusty amphitheater. Maybe a hundred people are sitting listening to the music, though the place could hold a few thousand. There's a kind of jazz fusion band playing: guitar, bass, drums; many amplifiers. "This guy's a tribal from Orissa," says my new friend, Siddhartha. "He uses up all his licks in the first song, but he has that look, that grace."

I'm up next, feeling a bit out of place on the big concrete stage. They plug in my background tapes—walruses and Weddell seals, icecaps melting, now all running through some bad distortion. I'm speaking a language as unintelligible as the script above the stage. The clarinet sounds like a Hendrix guitar blaring out of some 360-degree megaphone like the ones recorded mullahs use to call up Allah.

I've got my DAT cued up, it's digitally rolling. It's the beat and the accompaniment for speaking some phrases from the Upanishads on how we open up our senses and finally dissolve. How will it play in India, where the words first arrived from? We'll see.

He has become one
they say
he does not see.

He has become one
they say
he does not smell.

He has become one
they say
he does not taste.

He has become one
they say
he does not speak.

He has become one
they say
he does not hear.

He has become one
they say
he does not touch.

He has become one
they say
he does not think.

He has become one
they say
he does not know.

They say
the beat of his heart
it glows,

they say,
and by that glowing light
the self itself departs.

It goes through the eyes,
they say,
it goes through the skull

it goes through the breath
it goes through the face.

We don't see it go
we don't see it flow.
Will you miss it when it's gone?

Then the rhythm kicks in, soloing over the pulsing beat, now sounding so simple after these days amid the fervent drumming of south India. Soon I notice some backup sounds I don't expect. It's Siddhartha, who's plugged in a bass guitar and has started providing some aleatoric backup. Luckily, I'm no perfectionist. The music sounds, honestly, like it's never sounded before. The words go on, now containing a question posed by Primo Levi:

Is it better to live our tomorrows alone?

and then a spinoff from two strangely raplike lines by A. R. Ammons:

I'll tell you, in my way, the best way that I can.
I may be understood there *where I do not understand.*
I may be understood there where I do not understand.
You'll remember certain phrases as you walk past on the land.
As I come at you in phases as my time gets stuck in sand.
And the temperature then rises why I do not understand.
Like a clock under water, never set by the hand.
I may be understood then why I do not understand.

And then the tape is cranked up, the beat faster and more complex, the roar of the pulse and of the strained loudspeakers, the nascent distortion, that scratchy sound like that Hindi "flim" music you hear everywhere on the boulevards here, third worlding it, yes, I feel drawn into the image, far from my own rules, adrift in the world, finally able to fit in. Global pillage or global village? The crowd . . . well, the crowd isn't sure what hit them.

"He has become one," they say. I may be understood there where I do not understand. We reach the audience without knowing exactly how, or with what. Something goes on in ourselves with music and out to the world through sound, expressed, never wholly planned. How much of our self goes with it? Hopefully enough to make what's heard personal and real, but not so much that at the end we emerge spent and alone.

Do these words make any more or less sense in the land of karma, where we're all responsible lifetime after lifetime for our recurring, reverberant actions? I never got a chance to ask anyone. The rhythms, I reckon, were always much more clear than the language.

After the set, Sid introduces me to two of his friends, a dark, bright-eyed woman named Geetha—"She plays the *veena,* sometimes traditional, sometimes on Grateful Dead songs," he tells me, and she smiles—and her husband, Gopal, the other organizer of these shows, a guitarist. He's on next, singing above rhythmic folk guitar a sacred chant: "Suuuubrraaaamaaaaahniaaaaaaahm." He's an irrigation engineer by day. "The water," he tells me, "is nowhere near as dangerous here as you foreigners think it is."

After the show is done some people appear as if by magic, wait until all the equipment is packed up, and quietly go to sleep at the back of the stage. "It's their home," says Gopal offhandedly. Later, over mudlike brown curry at a local dive called Fish and Chips, he confides to me: "We only play untouchable rhythms. A bit like reggae. Makes our parents *really* mad."

It's easy to be deafened by the din that is India, but after a week you just want to join in with the surge. The air is polluted into a thick brown haze. To drive a car means you have to toot the horn; on the back of the trucks, painted in a usually bright color, are the words "Horn Please!" There is a music in these auto sounds, one quite different from that of the mockingbird-like car alarms of home. Those are lone bleats crying out for security, whereas here in Bangalore it's the mélange, the group yell, the crowded confusion of humanity making noise with machines. We are part of the fray, in it together, sharing the noise of the streets more honestly than the dream of peace and quiet. Even in the countryside there are loud screams: monkeys howling in trees, screeching birds alight over marshes; the snap of the jaw of a huge crocodile as it flips and swims deep to avoid your boat; the soft padding footstep of a brown bear on a leash.

The entire country is alive with color, history, possibility. You love it as soon as you lose your fear of the other and the illusion of control. The hard thing is to connect the chaos of this energy to the calm, grounding twang of the ancient music. I may be naive, but I imagine the music is not an escape from the mess and the sound, but something that makes sense most only *in* that boisterous environment. Hold to the solid drone and the overstepping rhythms. Use them as a backup to the hullabaloo. The single drone gives a ground to all sounds, and the beat makes you think that your traveling has some kind of order.

Every journey provides a superficial picture, every strange music can open itself up to you only a tiny bit. I will never grasp India or its music from within, and any attempt to find a new musical ground between mine and it will be like crossing a bridge, thin and high, over an abyss of impossible understanding, with no clear way to tell the good from the bad. An interesting place to be, trapped between one sense of the world and another. Spend enough time up there, and it becomes hard to know how to fit in anywhere. I dream of a standard to make sense of the blend, but no rules are likely to come.

Once home, it takes weeks for the energy from that experience to subside. It inhabits my dreams, while outside the winter is quiet and still. I keep this energy inside, put it into music, take months to garble it all into words. I put it together, mix and match, cut and paste it into a piece that keeps the thrum moving steadily on. The fire lives, the world must remain diverse even as distances between worlds decrease. Listen up if you are wont to forget: above the beat there are many stories still to tell. The drums are still pounding, the drone digs deep down. The music and the life do not stop. This wild world will surely endure.

THE THOUGHT AND THE STORY

Lee Konitz told me once that a jazz solo has got to tell a story. By now I'm inclined to disagree: as I've said above, music is not quite a language, and that's why we can understand, make sense of, glom on to the exotic, the strange, and perhaps inside it find some core of our own being. I have chosen certain accessible, alluring, but foreign scales, different but danceable rhythms, enharmonic but enrapturing sounds, from the world's cultures and from the natural world, to find a possible music, to create it on the fly. This is how improvisation makes up its own tradition as it goes along.

We also make our selves up as we go along, finding our way through the mass of conflicting advice and information that is reality. The better self is the one that admits the relevance of wide and distant influences, that is not afraid to bend its course to what it likes and find an original pathway through it all. We will meet many people along the way, in brief or sustained encounters. Many stories will be told, through sound, words, actions. No one story can encompass it all.

"So," I am often asked, "are you interested in the truth of this journey through music to the self? Or are you just interested in the story?" Music is no story, nor is it even a backup to the story. It is not the soundtrack of our lives but the *soundscape of life,* the philophonic joy of listening outward, hearing the ineffable through the specific, going beyond what anyone is trying to tell you to learn more of what is actually there. I know, I endlessly favor abstractions over specifics, but somehow I believe the truth to lie somewhere in between. Connect these words to your own specifics, your own stories.

Meanwhile, I want to tell you some stories—for without stories, as I heard Barry Lopez once say, we would die. That might seem extreme, but it is the stories that make us human. Science, technology, all our edifices, they rise and fall, come and go, but stories are the longest-lasting human works on the planet so far. (We'll have to wait and see what the future tells us about nuclear waste.) Music certainly doesn't last as long. Today, experts pore over accounts of ancient Greek music trying to envision what it sounded like, the descriptions of the instruments and tones remaining strangely ungraspable. Words can never replace or subsume the music, never pinpoint its power; instead they seem merely to ride on its rhythms.

Tell a story in words. Then try to tell the same story without words, only with sounds. Then try to blend the words with the sounds. Speak them, sing them: does this demand new music? How does the music change meaning when all of a sudden language is present? Hear the music, improvise a story. Hear the story, make up sudden melodies to go along.

Here I'll consider stories that go with music, perhaps ones about music or that work well spoken on top of music. Sam Shepard once said that any culture that starts to separate its poetry from its music is on its way out. I'm not sure where he got that notion, but our compartmentalized culture sure wants to keep the two apart, except in the realm of popular music, which may be the most powerful example of poetry being linked to music these days. But it shouldn't be the only one. Words complement music, have their own music; they may leave space for music or decide for the listener what the music will be about. I prefer them spoken or intoned to sung, existing separately but together, not competing.

My teacher the late Ivan Tcherepnin was troubled by the addition of words to music—he felt that it brought specific meaning to the pure sounds, firming over their rich ambiguity such that immediately the music becomes a backup. I disagree. If the mix is subtle, the two forces can independently prevail. Stories must leave space. Music must admit silence. Words can accompany music as explanation, as clues to refer to if more information is needed.

The best stories are nearly eternal, changing only subtly as people tell them again and again over the centuries. I wonder, though, what they have to do with improvisation, which is perhaps the opposite of the long-remembered story, more the sudden poetic outburst, the instant coagulation of raw material that may have been swimming wildly in the brain for years or plucked suddenly out of thin air. I am reminded of the brilliant Ben Katchor's cartoon series "Julius Knipl, Real Estate Photographer," about a shadowy character from the better past who roams the streets chronicling the surreal but mundane. In one strip a famous lecturer gives talks to hundreds of people who eagerly pile in from the streets, full of anticipation. What does he talk about? That's just it: until the moment he steps to the podium, no one knows, not even him. The man's an improviser, brilliantly impromptu with words. How does he prepare? Each week the books on his shelf are replaced with a random assortment of remaindered bestsellers, classics, reference works, and so forth, which he devours. Never stuck in one place, he is always ready for whatever comes next. He is training to be spontaneous. Absurd, but realistic: for what is conversation other than improvisation? What is being able to create a sudden story out of thin air and captivate your audience, whether one person or thousands, with the sudden glitter of your words? What is music?

Don't just tell your own stories. Overlay the world's stories upon the immediate moment, the present pulse of sound. Words have their own contour, melodies their own story. Ivan's trepidation has a point, in the sense of making each take on the characteristics of the other. Of course songs are wonderful, but speaking and playing allow both words and music to maintain separate identities as they live together.

Why combine them then? To confuse the listener? To add some specific tale to the vague rumblings of art? The kind of music I favor is the groove of the world, the scales that approach the universal but bend just beyond what is expected, that can go on and on without beginning and end. They create landscapes, set moods. There is room inside them for stories.

Some songs matter because they were heard at times in people's lives when music seemed to matter more than anything else. Some rhythms recall a special dance step from years ago.

Some music cries out for a story. The improviser, however, is caught in a paradox, wanting to tell a story but not to let it become a story he already knows. He wants to invent but not to lie. He is happiest when he surprises himself by accomplishing something he didn't know he had in him.

There are many ways to prepare for this instant, to hone your skills. You can practice patterns of notes and rhythms up and down, around and around, in every possible permutation and key. When you perform, though, you must forget all that, lest what comes out be perceived as mere exercising or showing off. Virtuosity has little to do with the power of the story. Indeed, it must be buried beneath the story so that no one notices it, buoying the action so the passion and uniqueness can come through. Learn all the tricks so that they become second nature, part of the vocabulary, the words that are not words, the phrases that mean only themselves.

More useful may be simply to go outside. Out into the world: into the woods, perhaps, where trees bend in the wind and the rain pelts an endlessly inventive music against the forest's measures, where the whoosh of the breeze across a lake is never exactly the same. Or go outside one's culture, one's traditions. There are patterns and rhythms to be found everywhere, ones that don't quite repeat but nevertheless possess an exactness that can be uncovered only in interpretation.

Think how hard nature films struggle to fit the world of nature into a storyboard. It's all cut and pasted to make the processes of the real world fit a human attention span: Here is the quail family, and now the owl swoops down for the kill. Yet something else besides drama may be going on. Accident. Chance encounter. Wandering. Travel. In human hands, however, aimlessness becomes significance, nature remains more than what we can see or extract from it.

Improvisations are often praised when they sound like they were planned out. Yet in my mind they work better if they capture that inherent spontaneity that lurks in all things. If, thanks to the music, the rain makes just a little more sense when next you are caught in a sudden downpour. The suddenness is all—otherwise you could save yourself the adventure of getting wet. But wouldn't that be missing the point? Don't be content to sit happily distant and dry.

Some stories, too, though carefully worked out, sound as if they were made up on the spot. I think, for example, of the collection of traditional Indian tales known as *The Panchatantra,* all parables designed to teach us one thing or another. A story might begin with a lion conferring with an elephant, unsure which way to turn in the forest, and they stop and the lion says to the elephant, "That reminds me of a story . . . ," and then we're treated to a tale about a monkey and an ibis who are working something out, but that story stops in the middle when the ibis says to the monkey, "That reminds me of a story . . . " And so one story drifts into another and then another, and what is remarkable is that you *never* get back to the original, framing, story, you never find out if the lion and the elephant find their way out of the forest.

What is the point of all this layered lack of resolution? I believe that life is actually more like the world portrayed in these stories than it is like our usual neat constructions with their beginnings and ends. Here, art emulates nature, eschewing formula and structure in the name of the open, the inexhaustible, the unboundable possibility of the story that can always go in a different direction, even when it is supposedly done.

I am drawn to stories that work like improvised music, and stories that go with such music, maybe framing the openness, maybe raising more questions than they answer. Throughout this book I've given examples of words that were spoken along with music, spoken independently rather than in song. In this attempt to define a certain kind of improvised, improvising, or improvisable story, you might finally see why certain words were chosen over others. There is no easy destiny to this expanding tale.

Parables, visions, excerpts of the unslakable truth can be found anywhere. We hold on to those stories that resonate with what we need, stories that can come from everywhere. That is how we melt into a wide, complex world. It's how we forget where we come from and find an identity through the things we love. Use those stories to create your own stories out of the rhythms you hear and the need to fit in.

I find plenty of seemingly improvised stories in the tales of my ancestors. These stories, in their tendency to jump from one place to another, have a feel of immediacy, a studied grasp of the suddenness that keeps the world in motion and adrift. Judaism is a religion of stories, often not stories with a clear moral, but that turn questions back on themselves. Think of the rebbe on his deathbed, surrounded by his faithful followers who mine him for wisdom. "Rabbi," one asks, "what is the meaning of life? Please, you don't have much time left on this earth. Could you tell us please?" The old master shudders and coughs a bit. "Life . . . ," he mutters, eyes wide and fervent, "is like . . . "—all around him his students draw closer, striving to make out his words—"is like a bagel." "What?" "Huh?" "What did he say?" whispers the crowd. "He said . . . uh, life is like a *bagel*." "A *bagel?*" "What?" "Why?" "Where?" and the murmurs reach on and out to the edges of the crowd, where a little boy is tugging on his father's coat. "Daddy, daddy, what did he say?" "Well son, he said, life is like a, er, bagel." "A *bagel?* What does that mean?" asks the boy. And the question makes its way back, as in a game of telephone, to the center of the crowd, back to the source. . . .

Well, we'll return to that story in a while. These stories work best when nested one in another.

In the eighteenth century, a mystical sect arose within Judaism known as Hasidism. In the villages of eastern Europe, in territory now held by Poland and Russia, music, chant, parable, and ritual were used to emphasize the ecstatic and extreme path that must be followed to serve the Creator. Although Jews are often thought of as an urban people, many of these stories display a particular attentiveness to the natural world. They do not admonish, they do not moralize, rather they connect the teller and listener to the surrounding world in enigmatic ways. Remember the heart of the world yearning for the fountain, a parable for ecstatic longing. When I come across stories like that one, I feel a pang of recognition for the tradition I am supposed to have come from.

Judaism, though perhaps now, after many centuries, urban and mercantile, was once rural, pastoral. Nature was home. Now it is passed through and marked only on journeys, as Jews wander across a homeless earth. We have needed to find a reason for our presence here, in order to keep some link to the tradition as we veer from it beyond belief. The strongest traditions are those that can admit change, that can embrace deviation as development, not escape.

How can music guide a spiritual quest? Here is another of Reb Nachman's tales, one that moves from situation to situation like *The Panchatantra;* in it, the ability to make a strange music that comes from knowing the world's more-than-human sounds is defended.

> There was once a man who could imitate the sound of any creature on Earth with his voice. People admired him, but they wondered, "What good is this skill? What benefit can possibly come from singing so strangely and so comprehensively?" The man then told this story:

"There are two countries, which lie a thousand miles apart. When night comes over these countries there comes a strange moaning, a wailing, as the very stones seem to groan and weep. People can't fall asleep. When they hear this sound, they too begin to moan and weep. Every night all the men, women, and even the children lie awake crying with the sorrow that sweeps over them. I traveled to these countries because I hoped to be able to ease their suffering.

"I came to the first country, and that first night I heard the strange cries. All of us, even myself, could not stop from weeping and there seemed nothing that could be done.

"But with all my experience of the sounds of the world, I could explain to them where the sound came from.

"Once, I told them, there were two beautiful birds that were mated together, the last two of their kind. They got separated from each other in a stiff wind, and they flew everywhere, each seeking its mate, until they became weary and lost all hope. Each settled alone where it was, building separate nests a thousand miles away from the other. Now when night comes, the two birds begin to cry, and the cry catches on to the earth itself, and careens onward without rest again and again.

"I told them: 'Take me to a place that is neither one land nor the other, but in the middle, exactly between the two. From that place I will send the sound of his voice to her, and the sound of her voice to him, as we can imitate all sounds in the world and send them as far away or as close as we like. Each will hear the other's voice as if right in front of them, they will listen, and tremble, and rise and spread their wings to fly straight toward the place of the voice, and they will meet together where I stand.'

"The place they took me was in a forest, the ground was covered with snow. I called, yet could hear nothing above us, as the sound had been transmitted just far enough away. Soon there were two pairs of wings above us. I had brought the two birds together, and the endless cries of the earth were gone, and the people and the birds could rest together at last."

You see it in the stories, you hear it in the songs: a deep, searching melancholy that seems to know no end, always pushing on,
always yearning. Wordlessly, Hasidism offers the *nigun,* the mystic
song without text, a searching prayer that never quite seems to end,
using music to push our thought forward and answer to the
rhythms of time and the earth. Here is what Reb Nachman had to
say about the purpose of this kind of music:

> And through the Tzaddik's *nigun,*
> when in him tongue-tied Moses sings,
> all lost souls rise from the abyss,
> find their way from the void.
> All tunes are re-absorbed in the song of silence,
> all heresy integrated and dissolved,
> tune and word, in the *thought song.*

These are melodies whose form has been altered so that they never
resolve, so that they continue to raise questions that will not be removed by easy answers. The music contains ideas, even though it
has no words. It is the improvised call that brings the suffering nations together, the sound that brings the lovelorn birds back to the
same place at last. Inside the unending surge of melody lies the
heart of the question that will not leave our minds: How do we best
serve the world that God has given us?

How to listen, how to partake? How, as travelers, can we make
sense of the details and blend them together into a coherent whole?
Perhaps if we move to a story that improvises its way from symbol
to symbol, that begins in one place and ends somewhere far away,
and does not return to its original questions. Play with the story's
possible directions as it goes, as it advances with surprises. Pay
attention to those moments of surprise. Keep the value of confusion with you as the story moves along.

> Far up in the mountains, beyond the last house, lived the wisest of men.
> He lived his days singing the joys of the world and the joys of heaven.

Whenever he came down from the mountains, he would walk through the streets of town and ask those whom he met what it was they lived for. Some would answer, "To eat and to drink," others would say, "To die."

"Come with me," said the Master. "I will show you how to live." And one by one he brought people to the forest. They swam, they sang, they worshipped with pure joy. They did not want to go back.

Back in the world of men, though, those left behind started to figure it out: here was a master who caused people to leave their families and forsake the pain of reality. It was clear: he must be captured.

But he was hard to catch. He always traveled in disguise. No one knew he was the Master until he decided it was time to show himself. *That was before the wind that overturned the world. The wind, the air, the rise, the fall. That was the time when everything got all switched around.* He was up in the mountains telling more of his stories:

Can you believe it? There was a strange kingdom where people believed only in money. A man was judged according to how much money he possessed. Those who had no money called themselves dogs, or birds. Those with some money called themselves men. Those with more money called themselves kings. No one wanted anything else but to get rich. Can you imagine such a place? *Before the wind that raged over the world. The air, the rain, the thunder, and more. Before everything got all switched around.*

The Master heard of this place and said, "Hey, let's go win the people from their folly. We can change that place around." They spoke to a dog, who would not speak to them. They tried then a mule, who had nothing to say. Even a sparrow, one with nothing at all in this place, would not give them the time of day. The sparrow said, "We've no time for your prayers. A powerful warrior is approaching our land. We know not what to do. He will take over our country and steal all our gold." *The wind, the air, the twist of the world. That was before, that was before.*

Marching across the mountains, down from the clouds, came a warrior, who had no use for money, or for happiness. All he wanted was power, to rule the world. His army would kill any and all that it found in its path. Money could not stop him. Wise questions could not stop him. The sparrows and cattle raced off in search of gold, so that they might rise up and matter, and be counted. "Money is everything. Cash is power. Power is status"—all this they said.

"Foolish creatures," said the Master. "There is only one God. He does not care whether you are rich or poor. Only he can stop the marauding warrior." And he began another story. *It was from the time before the wind. The wind that overturned the world. Listen up, listen good:*

Long ago I served in the court of a king. There was also a warrior in the council. He and I were best of friends. *Then the wind came and tore the world asunder: the ocean became a desert, the mountains washed away, the whole kingdom was no more.* I could no longer find my place. Everyone was lost. The warrior and the wise man were cast away from the city, along with the rest of the court.

I think this warrior may be the same man. If this is he, no one can stand against him because he is devoted to the way of the sword and will use it to vanquish all who stand in his path.

Soon the warrior was fifty miles from the city. He sent his messengers to demand that the city surrender. The money-worshippers ran to the Master and said, "If this man is really your friend the hero, isn't there something you can do?"

The Master said, "Will he not take your money?"

The people chattered, "He refuses it. It is nothing to him."

The Master headed out to meet the approaching armies. He met the warrior. Of course it was his friend, also adrift in the world, unable to find his place anywhere, driven to conquer, and always victorious.

"What can we do with the people of this country?" asked the Master. "They worship only riches."

"The only way to rid people of the love of money is the way of the sword," said the warrior.

Then the Master said, "That is true. You must go the way of the sword, and there you will find a path that turns and leads to a flaming mountain. But the flaming mountain is invisible, and on its top is a place where the most delectable of foods are prepared. It is far from the mountain, yet it is fed by the mountain's fire. But there is no fire in the hearth, and the hearth is invisible. You will know you have reached it by the two great birds that stand and fan the fire with the beating of their wings, making it rise and shrink as needed. Only these carefully cooked foods contain the power to make men forget the folly of gold. Lead them against the wind, and when they taste and smell these wondrous foods, they will forget the pull of riches."

So the warrior marched into the capital not with weapons but with the news of this quest. He led the people of wealth on this long, arduous journey, and they reached the sumptuous feast. After a few bites they sniffed strangely, turned around, and cried, "What is that horrible stench? Let us eat that delicious food!"

"It is your money that smells so foul," said the warrior. "Cast it aside, and you shall see the world as it is." They hurled the money from their pockets, the jewels from their necks and hands, and they turned around and saw that all men were equal, from sparrow and spider to elk and human being, and the world with its flaming mountains and distant fountains was alive with its own splendor, and all could appreciate it with simple worship of the God who made this place possible and actual, and there was much to sing about and to rejoice in.

And that Master, he knew it was time to return to his hideaway of joy and prayer. Those who were ready for such uplifting concentration went with him, but for the rest of us, we stayed and lived in society, waiting for our time for pious retreat to come. One day it will come to all of us, and we will then wander far, to the end of the world if we have to, until we find something worth searching for that long. *And the world changed slowly, gently, into a better place. There was no need for the tumultuous wind, and it never blew this way again.*

This story jumps from one platform to another, like a falcon soaring through clouds. It is buoyed by the repeating chorus of wind memory, the idea that something turned the world around, that the balance of things went upside down. The narrative doesn't need that wind—but there it is. It's meant to disorient you, to provide you with many strands of possibility but little information.

If I were to add music to this tale, I would begin with a groove of energy, standing for the Master's followers, who are having altogether too much fun and so become a joyous threat to society's toil. Then it would rise to another groove, steady like the oblique twists that move the story on. There would be glimmers of melody, hunting for the whole, inconclusive, searching, leaving space for improvised identity. Running in and around the story (or nonstory) would be the flurry of wind, the surge of air. Whispers. Hurrying. A rush to concede. But no easy way to finish because the music needs to continue asking questions even beyond its end.

Already the tale is like a suggestion of something it does not deliver on: some kind of wise lesson or an exacting path to a place you'll never be sure you've actually reached. Music can turn ambiguity into advantage. Listen for a song that squeezes exactness out of swirling uncertainty. Then create it, transform it, improvise it into existence.

Is life really like a bagel? So the little boy protests, asking, "Daddy, what does he mean by that?" The question reverberates back into the heart of the crowd, finally reaching the ailing old man. "What do I mean life is like a bagel? What do I mean? Okay, so life's not like a bagel." And then he dies.

You won't get anywhere by questioning the story. You must simply live with it, have it inside your mind filling the sky as you play.

If improvisation is to tell stories, the best results will be twisting, turning stories like these. The words, or the music, carefully inscribe possibility, not outcome. The stories you end up remembering will be ones that leave you room to breathe, space to create. Consider this tale from Zimbabwe:

There was a young mother who went to work in the fields.
She left her baby close by in a tree.
The baby cried; she could not keep working.
She couldn't get back to the fields,
as she kept going back to the child.

An eagle saw what was happening
and flew down over the field,
its great wings flapping down into the branches.
The eagle watched over the baby,
kept him safe, never let him cry.
The woman sowed seeds in the field.

At night she told her husband what had happened.
"Impossible!" he said, and went out the
next day to see for himself.
He saw the bird swoop down,
and he became afraid.
Frightened, he shot an arrow, aiming for the eagle.
The bird took off,
and the arrow killed the child.

Ever since that day,
murder has been in the world.

Ah, so that's why. Murder is in the world because we are afraid. We do not trust the animals to look after us, to consider our needs. We do not, for that matter, trust anything out of the ordinary, or anyone that seems different from us, anything we don't think we know. That's how animosity breeds. That's when tragedy strikes.

The story is simple, binding nature and humanity together to explain why people can be so cruel to one another. The words get inside me and I learn something every time I speak them. Although the tale is from Zimbabwe, I start to hear in it rhythms from North Africa, Berber rhythms, *gnawa* beats from Marrakesh. Da da *dum* da da *dum* da da *dum* da da *dum*, a pickup and a strong downbeat. One two one two one two. I put all the rhythms down out of disembodied electronic sounds and bring the tape in for the band to hear. Bill Douglass adds an acoustic grounding on bass, and Doug Quin places an eagle cry he recorded himself at the beginning of the piece, where you don't know what it means, and at the end, where you nod in knowing assent.

I am walking along a remote Maine island coastline when I spy a huge bird in a tree off in the distance. I say to my wife, "Let's walk slowly around this cove. Watch for that big bird in the tree when we get out there." We walk silently along the pure blue waters for about ten minutes. Then I'm peering up into the trees, looking for the one I was gazing at back around the bend. I find it, and there, at the top of this jack pine, is a young bald eagle. He's about a year old, still all brown from head to toe. He's staring at me, perplexed, unsure. On my chest is my own son, five months old. He's not yet paying attention to huge birds.

I hold contact with the huge raptor's eyes, admiring the talons and the powerful yellow bill. He adjusts himself on the branches, then alights, propelling himself with silent, slow flaps over the quiet sea, out to even more distant islands.

Baby, eagle, evening light. In remembering the moment, I have the story within me. Beauty opens wide. There is more than murder in the world.

In the previous chapter I mentioned the Swedish performance ensemble Lucky People Center, and how they had made a film offering up humanity as the dancing ape, singing and playing to the rhythms of the planet. On an earlier record they took on arresting political stories, and set them, montagelike, to a beat. These include the words of Rodney King ("Settin' these fires, it's not right, it's not going to change anything!") interspersed with the shouts of L.A. policemen ("Spread 'em out buddy! Way out! Back down on your knees!") and the cool comments of President Bush on the event ("I felt anger. I felt pain."). Another cut has Bishop Desmond Tutu explaining the African term *ubuuntu,* that sense of freedom that connects us to all other humans ("When one goes down, ultimately we all go down."). Another features the witnesses to the execution of convicted murderer Robert Harris in Florida in 1992 ("He winced a bit, and then he began to pant as he was suffocating.") interspersed with his own final words: "You can be a king, or a street sweeper, but everybody dances with the grim reaper."

The songs are cut-and-paste projects made up of real commentary on our wild world, held together by grooves and rhythms and smoothly pieced together sounds. The themes are freedom and its lack, and the astonishing kinds of cruelty human beings inflict on one another. What is exciting here is the way deep and compelling stories are revealed through fragments, enhanced by music that originates in a place far from where the stories played themselves out. When all are combined, though, the world seems a closer, more livable and inviting place.

Here, from their first record, *Welcome to Lucky People Center,* is the story of Nacho, who lived in a village on Nicaragua's Atlantic coast. One day he went to a nearby village to sell some fruit, and he was captured by the Contras, who took him as a prisoner back to their camp:

So they said to me, they said: "Nacho!
You shall be die, you shall be die!"
I said, "No problem, you shall kill me. It's no way then. I shall dead.
    I left my kids."

They went and they tie my hands up to a tree.
And a girl from Haloa come up to me.
They put her out to watch me. She said to me,

"Confidence me I confidence you." I said,

"What you can do for me?" She said,

"I free you for you to free me. You think you can free me?"

I told her, "Yes." I said, "Yes mon." She said to me,

"I can free you if you be with me . . ."

She went to work and she loose my hands.

She hand the gun in my hands, she said:

"Hold this!" I said, "I must hold this?" And she said,

"Yes, hold it." And we start to walk . . .

we walk on the beach, we walk we walk we walk.

I start to make a bark log, and into that I see a

sail coming, shooting, the sail coming faster then,

and I paddle, I paddle, I paddle, *brombom!*

Shooting! I told her, "Bend down!"

And they still continue shooting.

I told her, "Bend down!"

I told her, "Jump out!" And she jump out.

I said, "Hold on me!" And she hold on me.

And they still continue shooting.

I said, "Dive!" And she dive.

They left us. They couldn't catch us.

I come home here, and everybody

was nice to me.

Everything nice, everything nice . . .

It's an instant epic tale: the meaningless capture, the ultimatum from the girl, the wild alien English, almost dreamlike but at the same time very real. The piece (it is more immediate, more powerful than a "song") is called "Freedom!" and the word is shouted out over breaks in the rhythm, in and among pierces from the electric cello. The rhythm of Nacho's words, in turn, is carefully adjusted to fill spaces between the beat. Meanwhile, Nacho has returned, calmly, to his own world. What happened? Did the two live happily ever after? *Why* did it all happen?

Spoken words can be made to fit any kind of music, they can be overlaid upon any world of sound. Today cutting and pasting is as easy with sounds and images as it is with text. A new kind of story-telling goes with the new pastiche of music, with anything heard or captured on tape becoming raw material for the sound collage.

The hardest thing in all this is to make sense of the juxtapositions. We see too much, hear too much, but soon forget too much, readying ourselves for the next fix of amusement, allegory, or distraction. Does a good story need no music, or demand just the right music, or enhance *any* music you overlay it on?

Too much of the discussion about sampling in music has been about rights: who owns it, who should get the bucks for it. This approach isn't surprising given this most legalistic society in which we live. Yet I think it ignores the thing in itself. For most music, most art, is not about the marketplace, and might only incidentally make money. I'd rather ask why we choose a specific sound, what its qualities are—not where it comes from or who "owns" it.

I love Nacho's story. I love the way he tells it and its rich ambiguity. I've repeated it over and over again inside, trying to figure out why it interests me and wondering whether all the investigating is worth it. Not everyone shares my penchant for asking questions, even about the things I like. We are generally taught to admit that taste is personal preference and that the stuff worth debating must have absolutes behind it. But then we get the paradox: how can we tell good music from bad if we forget how to ask what the good in music really is?

I don't want to tell you what is good; I'd rather set the stage so you can ask and answer for yourself. Taste ought to come from reflection, following the initial allure. A musical composition or a story grabs you, and then if you ask why, you will learn a little more about what kind of person you are.

Sensitivity to sounds attunes you to artifice, but it also helps you hear the music in the world's stories. I've looped a short rhythm from a cricket's song, and I'm adding words upon it. I'm thinking black on white, caught with the winter image of a crow on snow. I'm playing the sound back over and over again, and the real crickets outside the window are getting wound up, all singing at once. I hear a thousand rhythms out the window, and my tape seems superfluous, until I realize this is exactly what I want: I want this music to fit into the world, with me in the middle, or perhaps off to the side—just somewhere in it. The black and white are oscillating in my mind at top speed like an inadvertent Rorschach; I want the image to mean more, to hint at some story that's not quite there. Black crow on white snow. It's appeared already in these pages—did you remember it? I still see him, not cawing, but silent, edgy, the opposite of camouflaged. Crow on snow:

a black crow on white snow
tell me what I need to know
about the silent things they said
about what happened in the bed
the night the feeling left you

it's time to tell me everything
just design it, do not sing—
some things do not sit comfortably in words
walk to the forest with them
listen in the company of birds

black crow on white snow
it's because of all that winter light
they all stand out

and always miss
the endlessness of night?

the crow's the shadow of those other birds
you think you're special, so unique?
we are one and all the same, while
there must be some mystique
inside your rightful name

we can never know
we will never show
too much about the black crow on white snow
its outline moves
the sun goes down
then stillness beams on this small town

white fades to black
down this long track
that glow we lack
until the hope of light—
it comes, it always comes
it comes, again.

It's supposed to sound incongruous, almost trite, not a poem but
a guide, looking for music to set it free. There are too many insect
rhythms in this autumn air, as I listen forward to the next season,
try to imagine it. I want to hear all the sounds, I want to know what
they all mean, I want to contribute to the fray in a way that will
get them to listen to me and not be afraid.

Freedom! We're all listening for it; all these stories sing of its possibility or its lack. Tension and great longing are its prerequisites;
we reach out so emphatically toward the world but are forced to
sing primarily of its uncertainties. For in the end, this magnificent
place might not be particularly interested in us. We must live with
this indifference nobly, not bitterly, keeping the faith in wonder

and telling the stories over and over, generation after generation. We must whip up ever new musics from the old, seeking out the eternal yet ever-changing rhythm to keep them instantaneous, new, exactly of its place and time, like no sound heard before yet something one can't imagine wasn't always there.

One reason to put the words away and express things suddenly in music is that language is so imprecise, so abstract. I latch on to these stories because I want them to stand for more than they are, to repeat them endlessly until they are ingrained into the firmament of culture. I'm afraid at times that the threads I find holding all these stories together are so thin that only I can see them. Music is precise, immanent, irrefutable, yet it says nothing specific about the world. It is music, pure and simple, an emotive outcry about sound and nothing more. At least, that's what they tell us. Yet I believe it is more than that: it is a form of communication that reaches out to the rest of the world. Animals and plants may also grasp it, unlike all that talk, which is utterly human and nothing more.

Why write about stories when you want to explain music? Because words are much easier to talk about in words. Sounds remain elusive, even as their rhythms and ecstasies engulf us. But the stories, see, the stories give the pulsing rhythms a human tinge, they are an oblique reflection for the sounds to bounce off of, a context. They start to explain things, but do not say too much. They leave room for the relentlessness of sound.

Sure I believe in writing words around music, or I wouldn't have begun this book. Yet these words must not define the music, though they might justify why the music will never consent to stay still. There are stories before the music, after the music, living around the music. There are words placed on top of the music, and words about the music that will never be uttered. The music ought to be full of ideas but irreducible to those ideas alone.

Improvisation embodies freedom, and yet it is a lot of work, always holding you down. Every moment you must be willing to invent something anew. You trust that your own inventiveness is endless, and you stay aware of all possibilities as you decide on just one. There is no need to give up on other roads, as in a calculated game of chess. Each true note includes all the harmonies that remain unsung.

The rhythms go on, your own contributions blend into the pulses of the other instruments, and the steadfast beat merges into the indefatigability of all the natural sounds coming down from the trees. You stop for a moment, but the music never will. You gasp, turn your head, add a few memories of a story that has lasted who knows how long through time. The words end, but the rhythms continue, and there is space for your sudden contribution that has never been heard before.

You cannot know what will emerge. All that preparation serves you well but does not predict the outcome. It's not chaos, but the way of nature, where a world fomenting without a grand plan can still end up exact, meticulous, deep, complex beyond belief.

Close your eyes, remember everything, then suddenly let it slip away and concentrate all your efforts on that illusion of being out of place, on that supreme human effort to fit back in to the place that set us in motion on this wild, uncontrollable path with still no end in sight.

Mix stories and music and you suddenly have a power that extends far beyond the words themselves. This power lies not only in the fleeting offerings of rhythm and release that music provides, but also in the act of playing. Musical instruments may be the most advanced technologies we have. They draw out of us emotions and forms of expression that we cannot even predict, that we cannot write down or explain. When the instrument works, it is a seamless extension of the mind, heart, and hand. As musicians, we forget it is there. We use it to get something out, something that cannot be trapped but that disappears as soon as it is heard. It is the poetry past words that moves only in sound.

To become comfortable enough with the tool that we forget it is there—this is an aspiration, the focus of hard work and a lot of time. Then again, sometimes it happens in a moment: we pick up an instrument and know it is right for us, that we are enhanced through its use without study or explanation.

The word *instrument* is so technical, so distant. Like *environment*, another term that no one likes but that we are forced to let stand in for that enveloping, embracing sense of the world we all feel.

When I say the tool extends me, I mean it is impossible for me to separate myself from the music the instrument allows me to make. I want the horn to be more than it could ever possibly be. Flute, clarinet, drum, sitar, on to the mythical and dreamy impossibles: shakuhachi, Samchillian Tip Tip Tip Cheeepeeeee.

All must seek until they find the tool that's right for them. You may pick up a mallet, bear down upon a marimba, and strike. The wood resounds. Or a pluck at a zither, a touch of the keys. When the sound leads you to forget all the excuses in the world for why not to play—how frivolous, how inconsequential, how little it matters to add to the bristling cacophony of the too much sound all around; when you've given up on excuses and need to add to the fray, you will know.

And then in an instant you might forget as well. Inspiration and necessity can fall away as quickly as they arrive.

Among all instruments, there ought to be one that itself includes all instruments, like that city that encompasses all cities, or that man I told of in the first chapter of this book who knows all the jokes of the world. He tells them not to make them unnecessary, but rather to surround them with a smile. It's an old idea, to emulate the possibilities of all sounds with one great mix. Church organs might well have been the first synthesizers, with their flute, brass, and string stops all created with a complicated mix of tones going through metal pipes. The great song of God should include all other songs, right? The synthesizer does the same thing, but with mysterious electronics that no one can see. And on the other side, we attempt to include all sounds in the most simple, as even a solo instrument or voice can reflect the world in a single tune or breath.

To what extent is music one thing, to what extent is it many? Think again of the noise of the world and the crash-and-burn release into a single sound. The question is not so much which instrument can do all this, but which instrument *must;* it's an issue of necessity in a world where there are too many choices to ever admit.

Some instruments are better than others. They are better in that they offer greater rewards through a greater time needed to master them. None is perfect, none can fully express what needs to come from the inside. Yet these tools help to create what is inside. Like all tools, we must be able to criticize our instrument even as we play it, even as we build it. The scrutiny should be heard in the music itself, as it explodes our instruments from the inside out.

My main instrument is the clarinet. What is special about it? It's a cylindrical tube of dark wood, the sound coming from a single reed vibrating at the end of the mouthpiece. Saxophones have a cone-shaped bore, flutes are played purely with air resonating through the tube. The physics of the clarinet leads to a special overtone structure, which in turn leads to that clear, clarified, woody sound. When you blow extra hard (overblow) on these other instruments, you go up one octave: an A becomes an a, a B a b, a C a c, and so on. But on a clarinet if you overblow an A, it becomes an e. A C becomes a g. And so on. So each octave requires a different fingering, which makes it initially somewhat confusing if you improvise. You could say, in other words, that the structure of the instrument leads to difference. On the clarinet, you play one melody, press the register key to enter the higher octave, and it's not an octave but an octave and a half: presto, your melody has moved. So it's easy for patterns to dance up and around, almost transposing themselves.

That emphasis on odd overtones, as opposed to all the overtones, such as the flute and the saxophone offer, leads to the famous woody sound. A flute might be made of wood, as a fife is, but not get quite that woody sound. This is the "clear" in *clari*net. That sound pierces through, mellifluous, crisp, somehow tubal—a crystal stream cascading over smooth banks of sandstone like a Catskill mountain river. Delicate but lucid, the thing has a preponderance to squeak, to squawk, to be too shrill. This may be why the clarinet has fallen out of favor. It could not compete with the saxophone as jazz got louder and more driving. Then when things get electrified, it proved very difficult to amplify, owing to another peculiarity: the sound comes out from all over the instrument, out of every hole. You can mike a flute right past the mouthpiece, giving it a surreal quality, loud and breathy. You can put a mike in a saxophone bell, and the tone will boom into the mix. But a clarinet needs two microphones to enter the electronic age evenly, one above the left-hand fingers, another off to the side of the bell. Blended together, they lead to the best balance. But even so, it's hard to crank up the sound too far.

So if you choose the clarinet as your instrument, you must turn down the volume, make a plea for delicacy. This is a bit of an anachronism in this ever louder age, though the instrument is still built for speed, that other accelerating virtue of our time. It's not hard to play fast on it, to dance up and down the scales. In New Orleans jazz it always filled in the blanks, moving over and around everything. In swing it was king. But now we are in another age.

I still see it, though, as an image for the human seeking a way into nature, for our dance among the world's colors and sounds. Flexible enough to bend and squeal, yet rigid enough to strive for the exact, the clarinet argues from its essence for a certain subtlety in responding to the sounds around it: it will never dominate, but may well reveal the beauty that has always been—like any inquisitive mind trying to find out about what surrounds us without destroying it.

The best instruments can take a lifetime to master, and they reward the constant devotion necessary to extend one's humanity into art through them. Other instruments, however, like the synthesizer or the CD player, serve to pull things out of us without much effort. The right tools change our music as it turns our good intentions into something better, something different from that which we could plan out or describe.

Yet as we follow the warm, meandering but clear path through the woody forest, close by we can't help but notice the angry shriek, the moaning feline noises, the unease and neurotic upset of the wrong notes, the off-kilter reed, the buzz, the worn-out breath unable to go on. To play well is work, and warmth will not survive if we insist on utter control. The depth of the instrument is revealed in its ambiguity, at least for those of us who are happiest when we are celebrating uncertainty.

How to link mastery with opportunity? Know enough, but not too much, so as to still be surprised by what comes out. Put yourself with your skills in unfamiliar situations and keep track of what emerges. Don't be afraid to *bend*, to slide in and out of the groove or the rules or the harmonies around you. That's what the clarinet is good at—dancing up and down through the ecology in which it finds itself. The more strange places you go, the more you will test the tenacity of who you are and what you know. That's why I try to be ready to play with anything, anyone, in any situation, no matter how unlikely. Hip-hop clarinet, country licorice-stick, adrift in India or in the midst of an ensemble of West African drums. Try anything once, but be sure to learn from what you do.

This is why I play along with cicadas, rivers, bellowing underwater seals, and crashing ocean waves. Words don't make human beings fit in to nature. The earth can't understand what we say, and it will eventually bowl over everything we do *to* it. But music, as I've said, is not a language; it communicates even when we don't know how it's doing it. It's a cry for meaning that lemmings and lemurs might hear. It offers us up to the more-than-human world.

The musical instrument, the tool itself, is part of this effort. It lets us do things we can't explain, extends our human essence through movement, the tactile rush, the power that comes when you move your hands, blow your air, or pucker your lips to release something into the world, something partly inside you and partly conjured through the machine. When it works, you're instantly more than yourself. If you're listening, you will not overpower the place you're in but will make your peace with it.

This doesn't mean you have to be quiet or tentative. I think of the bagpipe competition I once witnessed on the Isle of Skye. Pibrochs from dawn to dusk; long, ornate classical solo bagpipe concertos, for drone, chanter, and wind and gulls. The piper marches rigorously around a square, east, south, west, north. The drawn-out, rigorous cries shout humanity across the rocky moors. Try it inside four walls, and you've got something completely different.

Of course, different instruments make their sounds best in different places, different rooms, different volumes, and for different people. These days the boundaries all blur. More music than ever is available for perusal, at least at home, on disk or on the air or on the web. How are we to make sense of all the sound that is out there? We must listen widely, listen carefully, find our own pancultural pathways through the thick of it.

Modern arts broke many boundaries in the twentieth century, but one of the greatest contributions of art to our age has been its freeing of spirit, an emancipation that allowed us to listen, to look, to embrace and find beauty and intention in places that previously appeared unfinished. Red rock canyon walls or brick ruins that resemble Rothko canvases; microscopic crystals or wiring diagrams that seem straight from Mondrian's brush. There is an art in everything; we can feel joy just looking, just taking it all in. This is clearest in painting perhaps, but in music, too, people like Cage have taught us to love sound as sound, and all kinds of music have moved to celebrate the vast possibilities of tones and new ways to produce them.

Electronic music created a genre where music could be formed out of pure sound, through methods that continue to evolve. Less clear is the public's love for these sounds. The classical world by and large refuses to take such music seriously, claiming it to be shallow and artificial-sounding—even in a time when all recorded music, at least, could be considered electronic music, since it's been digitized and processed as bits and bytes and edited and carefully finessed on the computer to become a unit of information, where a copy of the original is "exactly as good as the original."

But that's a recording, you say, only a document of something real, the performance. There's some truth in that, for sure. The bagpipe extravaganza I mentioned would be very different if it were just a disk spinning above a laser beam, disembodied music coming out of speakers in my living room. For in reality it was an experience in an environment. Music is never only a pure creation of the composer made alone in the studio. As Rabindranath Tagore said nearly a century ago, "There has to be someone who hears." I would add: There has to be a world that the music fits into, a place it improves, an environment that invites us in through its enhancement, just as the listeners are drawn into the home of the sound.

We need to open up the boundaries between our instruments, between our genres, dissolve our sense of limitations and eagerly seek to bend the rules in order to create possibilities anew. Musical culture flourishes, advances, and transforms; it may enrage those who feel left by the wayside, but it nevertheless continues to show that humanity is not standing still. I'm not sure I'd call what is going on *progress,* but it is an opening up, a fabulous time of change.

A clarinet requires a lot of work to learn to play. Once learned, it makes a special and personal sound. Electronic instruments promise a plethora of sounds with input devices we're used to: now most often keyboards, but also guitars, facsimiles of clarinets called wind controllers, or black boxes that simply track the notes you play and turn them, player piano–like, into signals you can send to synthesizers that will emit any number of possible noises, some sounding just like acoustic instruments, others strange blends not possible in the acoustic world. Hundreds of sounds, waiting to be triggered any way you please.

Some feel the electronic instrument does not deserve years of practice, as such machines quickly become obsolete. How then, could one study them for decades? There is little need for virtuosity when it comes to playing the synthesizer. You press a key, and any of myriad sounds come out. Dancing up and down the scales is a lot easier than on the clarinet. You can do it for hours and expend little physical energy. Your body may appear to get tired, but only because it is used to the idea that making music is hard work.

This fact can be used to denigrate electronically produced music, or it can be used to lead us to think of this new, instantly available musical form as something outside the acoustic world, but outside in a useful and positive way. We can now produce any sound with ease, bending it, manipulating it, in ways that can be calculated and then described to the device. There is no longer the necessity to make just the sound the instrument was built to produce. Now we can take our intention, our way of playing, and separate it from the result.

But why do that? Either we now have that magical instrument that contains all instruments, or we have only the thousand empty opportunities that lead to the blasé world of five hundred broadcast channels and an infinity of easily reachable Internet sites, a virtual world of unclear choices, with little guidance on how to navigate them. It's all so new, so far from being finished, that the only way to explore these possibilities is to admit that you're unutterably lost and wander the countless pathways, whose number you only add to the moment you try to change anything, anything at all.

Electronic instruments offer you all the sounds in the world and plenty not of this world, but it offers them instantly at the press of a key. It's hard to resist, the access is so easy; it's like a shortcut to art, like taking a weekend workshop to achieve enlightenment. But once you possess all these sounds, after that initial feeling of power, as if you are in command of an orchestra, or of a session band plus guest players from all the planet's funky far-off cultures, then comes a sinking feeling: you have utterly no idea what to do with all these sounds, except to use them as flashy gimmicks to dress up the familiar.

Here's where the lesson of abstraction in painting can help. You must seek an aesthetic, learn to love the specific in the abstract. Listen—now all sounds, from the distant rumble of automobiles to a cow in the far field to a car alarm around the block, from a gasp in the neighboring apartment building at 2:00 A.M. to a wren in the roses or a gaggle heading south at the wrong time of year: all these sounds can be dissociated from their sources and turned into raw material. You can play irregularly and let the machine shift all your notes into an exact rhythmic grid (this is called quantizing); or you could play perfectly in time (just like a machine!) and tell the machine to *humanize* everything by shaking it all slightly out of place. So it might sound more human than you! Today's music machines can trip up or reign in our own sonic impulses.

A successful painting creates its own language of color and form. You like to look at it again and again because it reminds you of the possibilities that color, shape, line, and texture offer; it continually delights. Music has been called abstract for many more centuries than painting ever has. You listen over and over again, and when the music stops you may still hear it in the wind or in the screech of rubber in the rain.

I'm all for music that keeps us listening forever, long after it is done, listening for a place in the world that's right for us, where our aspirations, though bounded, seem limitless. So I ask to work like nature, to be admitted to nature, to find a way back into nature that also is part of the forward road. Sure, I'll use technology, even the latest technology, but I will insist that it too help us find a meaning for the organic that includes a way of playing and mixing completely artificial sounds, sounds that come from nowhere more real than a black electronic box. (Interestingly enough, in this new century these machines need not be black boxes, but often are bright-color see-throughs, glistening, curvaceous beasts that hark back to the streamliny future we used to have so much fun dreaming up in comic books and cartoons.)

How do you make a machine organic? Turn it off, go outside, walk through the woods or along beaches, down city streets, through factories, down alleys, and into dark, dripping caves. Listen, just listen, keep listening, and then try to make sense of what you hear. Make music outward; do not turn inward. Play from the world's living, cycling, moving possibilities. Don't just express yourself. The self is nothing without the place it belongs. And to save this Earth through music, try desperately to make sounds that seem to fit in, that point a way for us to hear our rightful place.

I question each instrument I consider playing to discover if it can produce a music that appears alive, breathing, moving, set off by me but surprising in its independence. I'll be connected to it only to the extent I'm connected to all living things: respecting the sounds that I make, in awe if they manage to assemble themselves into something beyond what I could have predicted. Musical instruments are good instruments if they allow us to create things we can't quite plan. Suddenly, new works well up out of us. They extend our sudden presence. It's up to you to choose which ones carry you to new heights.

Attempting to describe the process of choice at once betrays its dark side: I close my eyes and imagine a rush of intricate images, ten or more a second, like a flicker overload pointed straight at the brain. Images are worth nothing as currency; there are so many of them vying for our attention, and each season we're trained to imbibe them more voraciously as the technology speeds up and we zip them ever quicker across the globe over the invisible links that hold us all in check. As for sound, don't the media want it only as effect, to underscore, to accompany, the visual action? Who, then, has the time or interest to developed a refined sense of its reality?

The media are often thought to substitute artifice for real experience, but they actually work well when they serve to enhance experience. Walk through the midnight summer woods wearing headphones and a good stereo mike cranked way up. Bring it close to trees and grasses, and you will discover whole layers of insects undetectable with the naked ear. The technology even becomes an instrument when you learn how to place it and to move with it. It's an instrument for listening that can be pointed and framed, like a camera in the hands of a professional. But these days the camera is only the first tool used to wrest meaning from a captured image— now it's expected that the photo will be twisted, colored, flipped, given greater contrast, or otherwise digitally massaged, often simply because it *can* be done.

We only want to make these adjustments when the photograph is intended as art or advertisement, not as a reflection of what is actually in the world. The same goes for the sound you've brought home on tape or on a minidisk. Don't think about what it is, but rather about what it can become. Think about how you've extracted it from its home, left it empty of context; now it's your job to fit it back into a world. Don't use it just to make something seem alive, but use it to make music that is as real as a place, as pithy and dirty as an environment, as whole and admirable as an ecosystem.

Have you heard music like this? Have you ever wanted to? Or does what I'm saying seem like a complete departure from what matters in the whole art of sound? Music is abstract enough to be about almost anything, but for an honest environmentalist, one who wants ecology to be relevant to culture, art must resonate with the logic of interconnectedness; only then will it earn a place in the dream we're trying to articulate. I see glimpses of that art, that interconnectedness, in the anecdotes I've told, stories of chance encounters and sudden epiphanies in sound or in the circumstances surrounding sound. There ought to be possibilities for such moments in a world where musical tools are constantly being invented anew, but first we have to believe they are worth listening for and bend our attention to consider new ways they might appear.

Ever since his *Music for Airports* (1978), Brian Eno has been showing us that musical ambience can be found in more than Muzak or the muted tinkles of a cocktail-bar piano. Does music that is supposed to *be* landscape have to be a soft background soundtrack that is supposedly hip? Not necessarily. It will, however, be a music that creates a world rather than tells a story, music that might tell an ecological lesson by being part of a new, honest way of fitting in to the tenacious world.

These days Eno has been exploring the way recording music, placing it on disk as a fixed artwork, limits the lengths to which world-defining music can go. Yet in an age when sound can be ever more carefully manipulated, and CDs can contain not just fixed music but intricate interactive software, why not conceive of a music that is regenerated anew every time we hear it? In other words, why should a recording sound the same each time we play it? Each year, computer programs improve; surely by now, or at least soon, we should be able to create new music with every listening, such the composer, or perhaps the engineer or sound recordist, offers only part of the intention behind the work, providing not an exacting, final product, but only the raw material and instructions for completion.

Are you ready to give up control and let the machine mix and match your ideas? (Remember, we've only thought of music as a disk that you play in a fixed way any time you want for barely more than a century; before then, music was something you did together with others or else a printed sheet of notes.) If you are making not music but a world, you have to be willing to step back and let it flourish. That is how we find God in the details, not in the master plan. If you wish your music to be landscape, then you cannot expect to rule over it with absolute control. The real world is no place for a perfectionist. To fit in to that world, we must always do just a bit less with its resources than we wish. By not seeing the world as only something here for us to use, we sustain it with respect.

What artist wants to give up control to a machine that cannot think for itself? Remember, though: even though it can't think, it can help us to create flexible works that will continue to surprise us, help us to flow. It's not going to be easy, and it's not here yet. Art is not like a game of chess that can be won according to a list of rules. Out of the raw materials put in this flexible music machine must come something enticing if we are to consider it a success. It will be easier with sound than with other raw material because, again, music is not a language, and we love listening to sounds that we don't necessarily comprehend.

And eventually, when such music is common, maybe even the norm, our kids will look up, scratch their heads, and say, "You mean, Dad, when you were little, every time you played a record it sounded *the same?* How boring!" Then again, there are certain pleasures that future generations will no doubt lose interest in: a thundering operatic climax, soft music in a smoky jazz club way past closing time, the solo serenade of a *sarangi* minstrel in India. In the future there may well be more films and videos, more simulations of such events than the real experience. But the media never meant to substitute for reality! They've always been a form of entertainment, their goal to pull us away from ennui.

If a book is good, it is not because of the paper, binding, or typeface, but because of what you derive from it, what message lingers that you cannot shake. The same is true of music, if the listener is ready to take in what the art has to say.

But this is the age of endless possibility, with sounds quickly shifting one into another, even the oddest mixes no surprise. Maybe it's easier to create spontaneously this way, because, once attuned to the possibilities, you're ready for anything: no sudden switch jars the modern ear. Yet where is nature's ease, its flow, its rightness that's so easy to miss when it's gone astray? This natural world, too, can resound with bellows of confusion. We're more prepared than ever to take in the complexities that the world sings out.

We'll accept these technologies if they function in a manner that is transparent to our impulses as we work them—part of the ecology, part of nature, held together not by exact instructions but by a musical plan. Cut and paste; a wall of collages resounding through time; the straightforward documentation of recorded sound. It's all so simple, suddenly part of the environment. What is synthesized, what real? It's all on your platter; only taste will help you choose. But who has time to develop that when we're always after new ways to surprise?

Why would someone invent an instrument that bends the conventions most of us tacitly accept? The idea that what they've told us is tainted starts young.

I remember the first time I met Leon Gruenbaum. It was 1981. He invited me to his freshman dorm room to play me some tapes. Unusual scales, new tunings, computer-generated Bach chorales. "You can play these things in completely retempered scales," he said. "Nineteen notes to the octave. Twenty-eight. Forty-three. At first it sounds jarring, but with time you get used to it. You may prefer it. A lot of the piano's problems are solved." (You know the problems: every note is just a bit out of tune on the modern piano so that we can modulate easily from C-sharp to D and the chords sound more or less the same. We're used to it; no one complains.) The weird chorales Leon played for me were all churned out by a computer, and they sounded artificial and askew. That was a more primitive era of electronic music, when it was more often calculated than performed on the spot.

But never mind the weird electronic stuff Leon was playing for me. This guy could play higher on the clarinet than anyone I'd ever heard. Benny Goodman wowed 'em once with that super-high C at the end of "Sing, Sing, Sing," but that was just a midrange squeak as far as Leon was concerned. He could send a bell tone out at least a half-octave above that, maybe a full octave.

Once we took our two clarinets to the cavernous no-man's space beneath Le Corbusier's Carpenter Center for the Arts, Corbu's only building in the United States, a rambling concrete oddity whose official entrance high on a bridge could never be used for insurance reasons. There was this weird, dark, outdoor overhang space underneath the main studios that no one could figure out what to do with. The acoustics put a great echo on the clarinets. The woody tones would reverberate back and forth into a strange slap echo of the kind only concrete can produce. We riffed on Ornette's "Lonely

Woman" for hours. Leon actually knew the inchoate B-section of the tune that I usually chose to ignore. He showed me that it wasn't all that hard.

There's a whole generation of musicians today who grew up on Ornette Coleman. Yet as jazz becomes more and more a repertory music, narrowing its focus and shunning innovations since its late-fifties cutting-edge bebop peak, a lot of us feel out in the cold. We seem a part of no tradition, would-be innovators who wonder if we'll ever fit in. Ah, but it's a cop-out to be worrying about fitting in at this point. We all took the alternate path long ago.

I bring this up now because it seems that this popular lack of enthusiasm for the things Leon cared about drove him away from music, at least for a while. Who really wanted to hear those super-high notes, anyway? And who cared about the clarinet, a woody, squeaky instrument that seems out of place in an increasingly electronic world? Leon went on to study computers—something society could put to use, right? Those musical algorithms of his could at least find application in the tracking of information, the one and the zero, the client and the server, the node and the net. That was a safe direction, one "they" could approve of us going.

And so Leon disappeared into the maze. I heard nothing from him for years. Then a decade later, reports of Leon G. surfaced from the East Village in New York. They told me he was living on St. Marks Place, that his hair fell straight down to his knees. They said he was at work on an instrument of his own devising, with a name no one could ever remember.

One day in 1993 I ran into Leon right around Astor Place, and he took me to see his invention. "You want to know why I named this the Samchillian Tip Tip Tip Cheeepeeeee?" I was curious. "Just in case I'm ever interviewed about its history, you know, to prepare for a reporter to ask, 'How did you come up with the idea for the . . . er . . . SamCHILLian . . . um . . . Cheapy? Or is that Cheepie?'

'Yes, that's "Cheeepeeeee." Be sure to get the right number of e's in there.'"

The device in question is basically a computer keyboard connected directly to a synthesizer. Each key stands not for a note, but for an interval. So it's easy to play a lot of crazy arpeggios on the thing. In some ways it's reminiscent of that whole mess of round buttons on the back of some accordions. It looks very abstract to the uninitiated, but it's easy to feel once you get the hang of it. To produce a wild mélange of scales and jumps, just *tap tip tap* on the same keys and you'll rush up and down the octave, putting out a whirling cycle of fifth, fourths, thirds—whatever you set up. That's a lot of finger jiggling. But remember, every Samchiller comes with a free guide on how to survive carpal-tunnel syndrome. Don't try this at home!

Splatter the keyboard with a Jackson Pollock–style paint job, put it in the hands of a man with knee-length hair and the visage of a prophet, then set him loose on the downtown clubs. Now he's got a cult following. He's the odd man out in avant-funk bands. From the audience people are pounding their fists on the tables and shouting out, "Chillian! Chillian! Sam-*chill*ian!" as he rises up to take a querulous solo over the groove.

The Samchillian is actually a problematic instrument. The best thing about it is probably the picture of a wild character key-tapping away, his eyes closed, his chin raised in the air, fingertips vibrating over the computer keyboard, that spangled apparatus ubiquitous in our midst. His is brightly colored, and making a difference only by tossing and turning sounds in the air, not words, numbers, balances, or graphs. The Cheeepeeeee is best as a fist in the face of mundane commerce.

But as a musical instrument, it lacks dynamism, the sweep, the shape, of the phrase. An interval is only turned on or off, not shaped, blown, or plucked into place. The harpsichord and the pipe organ have the same problem, you might argue, and they sure have their place in the musical canon. Sure, but the computer keyboard is that much easier to click and release, that much easier to ruin your tendons on tip-tip-tipping away.

"I know, I know," says Leon. "Spare me your critique. I know it's a gimmick, but that's what people like about it." Give him an ovation, bring him back for more. What did you say that axe was called?

In a way, the earliest electronic instruments had some of the best qualities, ones that subsequent experiments have lost. Consider the theremin, for example, an instrument played by waving one's hands through the air. Its name was that of its inventor, Leon Theremin, a Russian émigré who was the toast of the New York 1920s avant-garde, but the name (a sort of cross between *thermos* and *vitamin*) was also strange enough to suggest that this bizarre instrument had arrived from the future. The theremin works roughly on the principle of those cheesy AM radios that whistle and shriek when you move closer to or farther from them. Attenuate that effect, and you have a sine tone that changes in pitch and volume depending on how you hold your hands in the air. You wave, you cut, you chop, you dance—all this real movement of the body affects the sound. Virtuosi (of which there are but few) can make a theremin sound as rich and expressive as a violin. Popularly, you may remember it as that sliding sound on the Beach Boys' "Good Vibrations," or as the dark menace underlying so many science fiction scenes from the fifties.

Given all the keyboard devices that treat musical sounds as things to be turned on and off, bent, and twisted a bit, the theremin had a certain exotic directness that has since been lost. Bob Moog, inventor of the synthesizer, is now back to making only theremins in his North Carolina studio, elegant-looking devices that he custom builds for any who want them. It's been said that the theremin was the first example of virtual reality, even with no computer involved: all you do is wave your hands in the air, and magical things happen. Sounds come out, and you can learn to control them. You can study, you can work, you can master the machine. Discipline required.

Like so much else, electronic music has become the province of information, not expression. But maybe the expression can happen outside the pure sound. That's what the Samchillian is about: it's not expressive; it's more about the show. But who needs expression anyway? The image is great: that erstwhile keyboard, artifact of our computer age, plugged into a black box and making all kinds of crazy noise. Crank it up, shake the speakers, push that disembodiment as far as it can go.

So why do our hands hurt? Why do we feel so tired when so little energy has been expended? All that cacophony scares us; we put our fingertips to the great calling for noise.

Turn around. Listen up, listen low. I do want you to make up your lives as you go along, to see all your experience as mere clues and practice for the endless recurrence of sudden music.

What kind of music is this guy talking about, anyway? It's an obscure music, of names and stories no one has heard of. He tells these stories that ramble and roam, he never talks about anyone famous but only about his friends, or what happened to him personally, and he tries to draw elaborate conclusions from brief accounts.

Now we have even more promises of instant sound, and virtual reams of web pages that will broadcast not only music but also noises of all shapes and kinds, so much specialized sound so easy to discover. Perhaps the instruments themselves will fade and matter less, and the world will reverberate and buzz and hum, and too much will be heard and not enough will be controlled, and things will get loose and wild and broadcast all at once — or just whenever you want, depending on how much you know.

It's all true, these things are happening and will continue to happen, as sure as that swath of mist will keep on rolling in over the meadow outside my window. Music is already even more virtual than previously thought possible, and soon all the sonic samples you need will be downloadable and remixable and redefinable and we'll all have to learn a lot more about how to mix and match. How immediate will be able to make all this, as opposed to the shout, the song, or the blow over the reed. Who really cares about the loss of directness, the reliance on the captured and tamed? Anyone out there but me?

Sonic art seems a self-contained world; it cannot be understood by figuring out what it sounds like. The danger in machine-made music is that we will disappear into the instruments' rules and systems, leaving our intentions unrealized and our songs without soul.

The music studio is usually a dark, cold place, soundproofed, with no echo, little sense of space. It exists entirely to be filled with artifice, for us to breathe life into the gleaming, frigid tools. On the opposite side of this image is the solitary walker out in the fields, playing a flute, trying to get a message through to birds. Sometimes they respond. They may take interest, and in any case are probably more interested in our music than our words. If we wish to capture this feeling later in the studio, we will either have to remember the moment very carefully

I have to think back twenty years to the first times I went out innocently to play with the natural world. Soprano saxophone against the pounding surf at Laguna, a smooth sound out into the thundering mists. I was barefoot in the water under the moon, looking down at the concentric circles of water and foam around my legs, seeking patterns, ideas, a score to read. And then came that enveloping fold of water thrumming down, a slow moving beat from south to north as the wave hit one place and then another. It was never exactly the same pattern. What could I, with my single small sound, hope to add to this complete symphony?

Then the same year, high in the Sierras, left alone in the forest to watch and count birds. During breaks I would transform the place I was supposed to collect data from, mess up the sample. Taking out a small pennywhistle, I would chirp and snip, trying to learn songs from the birds, songs that they might be interested in hearing me play. I'd change my style, think not of melodies or scales, but of bird things, go for the squeaks and the *chee-oop*s and the *pip pip pip pip snee*s. The birds were my public, and if I was going to play with them I would have to think in a whole different way about music. I would also have to stick to instruments that would let me forget about the self. For that is key: the idea that art is *not* about expressing the self, but about expressing something larger than the self, a way toward fitting in with the natural world that belies the human sense of separateness, inadvertence, and doubt. We can fit in, we must fit in, but to do so there is much that needs to change, and it may as well begin with a song that, while it might not appeal to a human, could well bring joy to a loon or a crow. I'll happily romanticize what other creatures might want from me, and seek out the tools that let us loose from our humanity, allow us to speak with unaccustomed wildness, get us into the wind and the seas, as we find our way to hollows in the soundscape that await our ideas. There are always such places, and that's what gives hope to the idea that there will always be room for human music, despite the world already being chock-full of our disturbances and our noise.

There is space out there, but still music draws us within. It is composed inside our heads, or rendered permanent on recording machines, machines that evolve faster than our abilities to listen or to absorb. Each trip to the recording studio seems to be a journey into an instrument that wants to include all instruments. The studio only partly succeeds in being this all-in-one instrument, however, because with its mixing boards and synthesizers and computers it reduces the physicality of making music, the release of sound through work into the air. The studio may be pure and clean, but it is far from reality. It is a place where much music is made today but that is set up as a retreat from the world. It is easy to forget what lies outside when you spend too much time there.

When you return to the surface, you hear everything in terms of the dials and devices you've been playing with. Is it the same with more direct instruments? Russell Sherman has written that to play the piano is to "consort with nature." In this most equally tempered of instruments, the consummate artist finds all possible variations in expression. But most players, even the best, rarely think their instrument is part of nature.

I want the instrument to transform me, to include me in the wider world. I want to use it to communicate outward, beyond the rules, to find a way of fitting into my surroundings. And then I want to know that instrument so well that I can forget it is there, and let raw expression come right through me. To work with nothing extraneous: no machines, no tools, no walls, no nature. Making darkness audible, making the doubt go away. To surround the sounds with words—as if words could explain anything. Because I still don't know where this music comes from, or where it will lead.

Why do I continue to prefer the improvised? There is no perfect instrument that includes all instruments. Our instruments start out anonymous, then prove their usefulness when individual people transform them. Then there is the sense of organic surprise, as if you're discovering life as it emerges and flows, following rules, to be sure, but also spontaneously inventing itself as it goes. No matter how much we learn about this process, in the biosphere or in the realm of aesthetics, we must marvel at it and keep hold of our sheer wonder at what has emerged and what's going to keep emerging until we give up. But to that I must also say: Don't give up.

How do we win an audience over to something new and strange? It's easy to see why the experimenting artist often fails to do this. She performs as if for herself alone, looking inward, mining the self for all it's worth, giving her all, but forgetting that the public must be lured in gently, won over and convinced that they really need something new. It's always an important moment when the self-involvement breaks down and the warmth of a performer comes through.

I think of my composition teacher Joe Maneri, long known at the New England Conservatory for his passion for microtonal music and his pure enthusiasm for breaking the rules. In recent years his career has been reborn as an international touring avant-garde jazz musician. Joe plays shrieky, emotional, weird music. I do find it hard to listen to his music on record. But live, he never fails to win over the audience. "My music is about *love*," he announces with all honesty before a set. "I love you, the public, so much, I have so much to give, I'm so happy up here playing." And those put off at first by the noise soon warm up and realize that this is an extraordinary man, a man full of joy who will walk through the crowd and *play* for each person one by one, really trying to please, truly astonishing listeners with his desire to communicate through the music—the improvised, the unpredictable, the immediately new that sings of the infinite possibility inherent in any moment of streaming sound.

The world loves music, and it does not question the worth of what a musician does. It's when we start *talking* about the art, about what it's supposed to mean, or when we claim that one music is better than another, that one music might have some positive social result—it's then that people get impatient. Isn't any music better than no music, they ask? Isn't the singing through sound simply a celebration that *always* makes the world a better place?

More music is available than ever before. You can own it, slap it on your machine, broadcast it, hear it in every public place. But just how much is it essentially woven into our lives? Henry Miller liked to think of himself as a park, a place where others in his orbit would come to rest and collect themselves for a time. I would like my *music* to be a place, a real place, yet not a place you can find on a map. A world of living sounds that have as much order and disorder as the natural world, following nature in that famous "manner of operation" that Aristotle, Coomaraswamy, Cage, Eno, and others of us have striven for. All of my work, from music to writing to conceptualizing, can be seen as an attempt to figure out just how nature operates aesthetically and how can we emulate it or learn from it in order to earn our place inside it.

I must stress again that *being natural is no easy task for the human.* Easy enough for a raccoon or a willow tree perhaps, but we people must work hard to earn our place in the living, breathing world. Whether the impediment is history or language or machines or our bicameral mind, who knows, but something has pulled us apart from the surroundings, making it easier to ignore the world around us than to strive to fit in with it. Art need not try to copy nature, but it should work hard to open up a place in nature for our songs—but by luring, never by imposing.

There have always been artists who have seen and heard nature as the greatest good, into which they hope their work will be fine enough to fit. The surrounding organic world is the most immanent and obvious locus for such a sense of rightness. Yet looking for artistic ideas in the shapes of mountains or the sound of falling leaves is a difficult path, because these world processes *do not need us.* They get along fine without our celebrations and our scrawls. Nature is the toughest audience there is.

The musical is not just a discipline but a way of perceiving the whole world. Words may be musical, life may be musical, the empty sky and tunes of blown leaves may be musical, if we learn how to perceive them. With music, we search for rhythm and relationship, a rare kind of order that is both explicable and forever beyond explanation. For we do not read the music of the earth, never mind the spheres, as a text or a story; rather, we hear it and are touched by its beauty without needing to understand it. Music is no universal language, but a blend of order and explanation in between rule and release, reason and emotion, plan and surprise.

Music is the art where sudden meaning can be invented, where immediate expression can take place. My concern is not how to create art without premeditation, but how to meditate oneself into appreciation of the wonderful immediacy of the world. To feel the unexpected, to notice what is impossible to grasp. My stories come out of life and out of art, as both problems and patterns, to become lessons of the spontaneous. What I have offered here is not a guide for how to let go, but a series of clues on how we might let the world construct itself in front of us, as we go. Let the plans slide, watch as they go awry: there will never be a lack of new discoveries to take their places.

To be a musician is to know the musicality in all life, to struggle to hear the constantly changing music not of any distant spheres, but of the immediate earth, without beginning, without perceivable end, a rolling improvisation whose lifting flight we can never catch up with.

When I say the world is improvising, that does not mean I listen and hear no plan, no order. What I mean is, there is no easy way to reckon a structure of beginning, middle, and end. In fact, the struggle is to learn to hear as music a sound world that does not cease, that has no initiation, no conclusion. You may learn to hear such as music by recognizing that there is also human music that has no beginning or end. And it may be true that most of the world's music is like that: When a group of musicians begins to play, they are tapping into a source that is already there. When they stop, they turn away from an ever-flowing composition that has no choice but to go on.

Music is the art of patterns, of design repetition, of rhythm in the recurrence of idea and change. To exist, it cannot stay in one place; it must move on.

Pick a day of strong, noisy weather and go outside. Wander straight into the ceaseless rain, at the height of autumn, as the bright leaves are wrenched from their branches by the weight of the water. The heavy sound of beating rain does not stop, but constantly changes. I wouldn't call it restful, I don't feel so secure, as it soaks our clothes to the skin and we grow colder and colder. But it is a continuous sound, one with constant variation, one forever inside us. It has always been possible, always raining even when the sun shines.

You will of course hear what you want in this tempest: Beethoven, gamelan, Debussy, Pink Floyd. Storms have always led straight into music, just as music confronts nature with its own range of rules and struggles to fit the tumult of natural variation into our limited sense of what we will "enjoy" listening to.

Rhythm isn't only something audible: it's also visible all around. The track of a yellow leaf blown through a forest of red; the concentric strokes of the wind on the water of an impeccably round, blueberry-ringed pond, as if some great animal under the surface is trying to push its way up toward the sky, fighting on, dancing out from the center.

Despite the drama of such events, there is also an underlying sameness to them, a reverberating thrum, a cycle to grasp on to. It is too composite even to hear, and I can't diagram it or sensibly explain it, but I am aware that it is there, a music of time that is as much a way of feeling the world as it is a way of playing it. Yet don't look only to musicians to interpret it. It is your choice as much as anyone's: you may hear the world as music, and tune into a place that convinces you that the best reason to live may be sung. Don't look for saving grace in a pretty tune, but learn to listen: only then will you be able to chart a course in and around the clouds. Sometimes you will hear through them, and sometimes they will block all the senses.

Chance can be a powerful guide to order, as any student of evolution will tell you. Invention rapidly leads to places you can't expect. The evolving sound around you may have no purpose beyond to tell you just where you are. Yet after a lifetime of unsettlement, that might be enough. And indeed, it is no easy goal: to hear just where you are, to understand what the rain hits to make those drops sound that particular way, to recognize the footsteps padding on the floor above, to know whose doors are slamming before dawn outside in the street. How else do we make sense of the birds flying south in flocks, or singing at odd and even hours, the ones that are in cages and the ones that flit from bush to bush in freedom? To *feel* each change as if it meant something—what would it mean to *hear* the light suddenly strike the brick wall across the street, after a long, restless, windy night? Even the ceaselessness of dark weather eventually ends. If there is an order to the change, if you sense a meaning, it is an improvised meaning, a sudden choice, a discovered art.

Yet it is rare that art looks like nature, sounds like nature, mirrors nature in any but the most mundane ways. When I first heard of *mimesis,* the idea that we humans in our drive to create were just trying to ape the infinite power of the creator, I didn't get it. Art was art, nature was nature, why should one ever be like the other? After years of walking toward the wilderness, still unsure whether I have ever actually been there, I at least feel the difficulty of trying to fit in. We do not easily know nature, and there may be no nature that wants us. But to feel at home, we have to let the world play upon us.

These words are all fragments of things heard before. The silences and sounds seem the hardest to describe, as even our language points to things and says "Look!," prejudiced toward the visual. Imagine instead a challenge of sounds, and then ask who will take charge and make sense of the stream and the peal.

Rain dripping all night in the gutters and from the roofs; now the sky is silent and fingers dance over plastic keys in the next room, forming virtual words on a screen. The two sounds are not all that dissimilar, both rhythmic tappings that surge and then fall, while down in the street every so often a car rolls by, then maybe there's the screech of old brakes on a truck or a bus—for this is right on Main Street in a small American town, a place where the full realm of sounds might possibly make sense. Looking up and tracing the ridge as it rises from the rooftops toward the rolling clouds over the mountain's summit, I can see a soft movement of tiny twigs and the trees' branch tips: not to hear the wind, but only to see its results. A delicate sound must be out there, muffled behind storm windows, fingering the air. Does it all hold together?

To hear the world you do not need much information. You need only believe there is something worth listening to. Turn off the music machines and hear everything around as a music in which each of us has a part to play, one at a time or in groups. What is the plan behind what is heard? What are its qualities, and how do we fit in?

At dawn I hear the strange blend of a whistling train heading north and a flock of geese going south. They meet right outside the window—or at least that's what it sounds like. All around this meeting the morning is silent. The sounds blur together, yet they have nothing whatsoever to do with each other, except that they cross right at this exact point. I'm startled awake, caught by the canceling out of opposite journeys.

Some philosophers have imagined that we sing the world into existence, wanting humanity to be essential to the world, though all evidence points to the contrary. How about listening to the world instead, hearing its presence, not insisting on our necessity but finding a way to be tolerated, finding a part to play, a reason to jam?

The geese fly against the path of the train, the chorus of this fluid arrow of voices countering the breathy high-pitched whistle and the grinding diesel engine, then there's the polyphonic screech of the brakes halting the lumbering metal. Can you always tell a natural sound from a human sound? I used to think so, but now I'm not so sure. There are birds in Australia that improvise concertos for their solo voice and insect orchestra; and in Java the cicadas sing a different song after the nightly gamelan performance is done. One listens for patterns, some sense of order to hold on to: the universe must have a plan, and if it's there we ought to be able to hear it.

There is a seventy-minute recording of nothing but the sound of spring peepers captured and then played back at different speeds. Repeating tones, audible cycles. Nature's minimalism sounds so much more alive than the machinelike repetitions of synthesizers or human musicians programmed to play like machines: even, exact, with no allowance for surprise construed as error.

Nature's amazing order is marked by imperfection. No wave crashes exactly when we expect it to, no snowflakes are alike, no one has enough words for snow, no sound is perfectly in tune with any other. No rhythm out there keeps perfect time. Birds sing for much more than simple communication. But why does the waterfall make music—does it sing if no one ever pauses to notice it? Who plans the tones, the arpeggios of the wild?

Out of the rush and roar of the world comes the search for a pattern. The biologist E. O. Wilson describes how scientists "[weave] ideas from old facts and fresh metaphors and the scrambled crazy images of things recently seen." So, too, does the musician. Yet after the pattern is found, the paths of scientist and musician diverge. The scientist needs to continue to explore, whereas the musician wants to find a way to keep the pattern present, to hear the continuity by turning it into something like the inspiring sound that is out there, something that will grab you, guide you, point you toward resonance with the world.

T. S. Eliot said we ought to be the music while the music lasts. The harder thing is to be the music after the music stops. That happens when you learn to listen to the world as music. I'm not sure whether this just makes life more interesting, or whether it teaches us a truer place in the planet. Think of John Cage, master of attunement, living in a sparse, Zen-like loft in downtown Manhattan. No music was ever played in that apartment. There was no sound system. There were no instruments. "Music?" He would smile, then raise the window, bringing the jarring sound of traffic and commerce wafting up into the room. "That's all the music I need." That part of town is being taken over by superstores today. But the noises are still there. Although Cage is no longer around and, like the best of teachers, did not train disciples, he did open us up to find our own paths.

I do not want to hear the din of the streets. I slam the window down, move to the country, listen for waterfalls, try to hear the sunrise. There is a comforting hum to be heard underneath everything, and it isn't the sixty-Hertz cycling of electricity or the whirr of the computer's cooling fan, nor is it my heartbeat or the swish of my blood circulating, or the tappings of feet on the floor above or below. It's the push of life, the lift of the moving river, which flows toward the sea, then is brought back by the tide. Always moving, never exactly the same. Know only enough about the patterns that you may still join in—by listening with care, or learning to play along.

Music brings comfort by bringing order to sound. But then, over time, it explodes its own rules. Do not decide what to hear or when to stop. There are no fixed parts in the orchestra of the world. This is how the sudden music, the improvised life, becomes something to look forward to. Think of the surrealist René Daumal, who saw his own writing as analogous to diagrams of true relationships that could never quite be expressed in words. Ludwig Wittgenstein, too, wrote that one could only talk around the most serious truths, never reveal them. Listen to the spaces between words. Listen even more closely to things that appear to make no sound at all.

The weaving track on the clifftop, the sense that the reflections remain even after the sun sets. Why is the sea so much calmer at night? (One scientist said, "Because we can't see the roughness"—not a good answer.) Remember landscapes and imagine how long they might last; remember, too, that no one really controls what will become of them.

The continuous and the moment. Our eyes and ears are touched by surprise: the sunbow only appears at exactly the correct angle between the viewer and the sun. The trail leads to a pond in the middle of nowhere. The leaves swirl into a perfect circle on the sidewalk. Every year it's the same and not the same. There's a single hawk holding place in the sky.

If you are captured by the sensibilities of music, you may struggle more to listen to the world than to impose order upon the possibilities of sound. And that may be the time to stop making music, to realize how little we can possibly know about the depth and meaning of even a single sound. The brilliant sitarist and guitarist Amit Chatterjee leaves a message on my machine: "You won't be hearing from me for a while. I can't play tempered music anymore." He's going back to his roots in the ways of pure sound, the resonance of the whole before the violence of fret and modulation. I call him back. "It's okay," I say. "I want to untemper the rules too." (Lately I hear he's relocated to Berlin. Somewhere, sometime, I'll run into him by accident and the rush of questions will well up once more.) The composer David Lumsdaine quit writing music when he heard the songs of the pied butcherbird at Spirey Creek in New South Wales. This bird was improvising concertos backed up by the whole ecology of the stream valley. Jazz saxophonists, worn out from playing too fast for too many years, retreat to the pure tones of the shakuhachi, with its singular, separate tones, each striving endlessly to evoke the purity of the wind struggling to sing. Either the purest music, or the opposite of music.

All these players are running, running away. They have heard too much, and forgotten how to listen. It's time to tune in to the world.

Change the world into music and you will do much more than you ever could on your own. Listen for constancy in the world, and you will hear change. Choose instead random implausibility and try to walk somewhere new, using the same strange method that allows life itself to evolve; you will retrace your tracks and discover new possibility.

I have sought to integrate the musical, the natural, and the improvised in my work. Could the earth itself be improvising, keeping time along its own rules, ones that no human will ever fully know? How, then, can we hope to be a part of it, to honestly join in? Perhaps the music itself, the very fact of improvisation, is the key, giving precise instructions on how to fit in to the scheme of things.

Recently a few writers have suggested that the fluid, surging, organized yet unwritten art of improvised music might have specific lessons for us as we try to address our environmental crisis.

The Norwegian ecophilosopher Sigmund Kvaløy went to New York in the sixties to study electronic music, but the sheer human domination of the place deterred him. Where was the surging pulse of nature in the great city? He found it in jazz, in those Cs against C-sharps of Thelonious Monk, in the organic movement and constant surprise. Jazz, though supposedly an urban music, works the way nature works! Perhaps here, in this aspect of the city, we might learn how to tune in to the accidental exactness of the real natural world.

Kvaløy asks us to imagine that we're playing in the back row of an orchestra, reading the score closely for forty-seven measures, waiting patiently for our turn to come in. The music is all planned out. We follow orders, the conductor guides us. It's the prison of mechanical civilization.

Sure, classical music also wants to emulate nature. Mendelssohn, Holst, Messiaen—there are many images of the wild in such music. But the writing down can lead to the freezing of inspiration. Look even at the avant-garde: Karlheinz Stockhausen once wrote of a piece that the flutes should at one point "play in the rhythm of the universe." "Mr. Stockhausen," asked the second flute, "how will I know when I am playing in the rhythm of the universe?" "Vell," glared the great composer, "I vill *tell* you."

Jazz at its best does not work that way. It's a give-and-take, where we know the rules and then break them. Acting in the moment, dancing to the time. It has happened before, but it will never happen again. It is *sudden* music, and if it works, the world ever after will not be the same.

Memory never encompasses change. The world lives on, and we make only a slight difference to it all. But if we can just catch a piece of the excitement, of the earth at its edgiest, moving, changing, singing to us and us singing back, then we have lived, then we have learned something worth saving.

The notion of jazz as a way of fitting in to the world surfaces time and again. Evan Eisenberg, for example, in his mammoth and fascinating *Ecology of Eden,* suggests that instead of trying to control nature, or worshipping it as an ultimate good, we should rather jam along with it: "Ditch your notated score—whether ascribed to nature or yourself—and learn to improvise. Respond as flexibly to nature as nature responds to you. Accept nature's freedom as the premise of your own: accept that both are grounded in a deeper necessity. Relax your rigid beat and learn to follow nature's rhythms —in other words, to swing." Listen to the moves of the world and you will know just what to do. Eisenberg calls this human approach to nature "earth jazz."

It may sound as if earth jazz is just an environmentalism of relaxation, where you don't take theories too seriously and refuse to be regimented by well-laid plans. More than that, though, it's a declaration of humility. The information's not available to the mortal man. When things don't work out the way we expect—and very often they won't—we must adjust, we must follow the flow. Learning as we go, we will not remake the world entirely in our own image. Instead we will learn to slip and slide along with it, to be just another part of nature, not its boss. A reflective, creative part of it, true, but still able to howl in astonishment like the coyote in the meadow by the light of the moon.

Now, is earth jazz a metaphor or a music? Eisenberg's image of slippin' and slidin' through complex problems is fine, but to improvise with our resources, with our planet, with our place, is not to throw all caution to the wind. There is no need to forsake our urge to plan, to see order. But things never work out just as we expect when it comes to seeing the world, and the world seeing us. We test, we play, we work our way into those rhythms and dances that are always going on all around. Jamming with the earth, figuratively or literally, is a way to find our place in it, and it's also a way to make music out of sounds that we might at first not notice.

I've used technology, cutting-and-pasting the wingbeats of insects, for example, into my mix. The patterns now have a meaning for me, even if I do not know what bugs are singing them. And why should that matter? Hearing is forgetting the name of the thing one hears. *Chh Chh Chh,* breath, *Chh Chh*—an August sound, a season's mark. Now it's part of the music inside me as well. Once I've caught the sound, I crave only discipline, or a way to place this music inside a tradition of other musics so I won't sing it entirely alone.

This book began with a chance encounter, and the suggestion that such accidental moments can be full of meaning, of inspiration for the taking of artistic chances. As the years go by I have a hunch it won't be enough just to improvise the changes of my life. I will always prefer the sudden music, but now it has become a music that begins with listening to the world. And that will allow me to co-create music with trees whose voices can barely be heard, to fit in to an environment where people and animals speak the same language, only it's not quite a language but a song that everyone knows a bit of while no one remembers the words. A smooth, warm feeling comes when the melody sweeps down upon us and the harmony emerges from the colors and shapes of the leaves on the ground.

Often I feel that music, when it works, has nothing to do with language at all, particularly the language used to bolster art when the art itself seems to dive into the clouds of uncertain genre and purpose. The art itself should convince you, and in its conviction and direction it should make you want to listen.

We can never spend enough effort learning to notice things. Only through greater attention to the songs of the world can we know what song *we* ought to sing. We may not be able to consume our way out of an ecological crisis by eating the right foods or buying the right clothes, but we can sing and dance our way toward the solution by listening and knowing just when to join in, and by learning that humanity cannot stop the endless music all around that wants us, that needs us, that is waiting for us.

It may be that the most earth jazz can teach us is to notice things, to listen to interactions: not simply to smile, enjoy, and take it all in as Cage and the soundscapers would have us do, but really to find a way to fit in—musically, culturally, individually, and collectively, to respond, to wend a way inward and outward at once.

No time has been so global and less local than ours. We must earn the right to be an animal, to have a habitat, to own a song. We must learn to let go even we learn to hold on. Music and philosophy are one. The song and the solution are one. There are no words to forget, no one melody to learn. There is a sensibility, a sound that meets all comers, a way of finding your niche, your route.

In Scandinavian languages there is a word, *musisere*—to "musify," to make everything musical by musically remaking a human place in the world. It's not as simple as singing along with the birds, and it's harder than composing a song. You can musicalize experience, treat all that happens as a moving, spontaneous, but somehow structured work of art. It's all improvised and new, but it has rules—bendable ones, to be sure—and evokes a tradition that defines itself only through the present right on to the future.

Maybe we shouldn't call this music "jazz" anymore, given all I've said. But what, then, is the rightful name for the world's total music that makes itself up only as it goes along? Maybe no one will play with me after all the criticism of self and others I've insisted on inflicting along with my art. But I hope in this new century not to be reduced to playing alone. The time and the turn of the time are too precious for that. You too can listen, and get ready to join in. I'm still afraid that I don't welcome the appearance of most music, perhaps because so much of it is designed to be put on in the background of our lives. Like most musicians, I have enough noise going on in my head as it is. The problem is to figure out which part of the inner thrum is worth giving voice to, worth putting out there in the hope that someone else might care.

Those few things I do like are not predictable. They glimmer accidentally from open windows, bass-heavy ghetto car stereos, endless remixes of the music of the past into the music of the future. Who knows where they come from? They are not from one kind of music or from another. They do sometimes sing of a natural world, a whole world where my song also might join in. I'm with the band, I have a place, I meld into the sounds, even if the song is complete as it is. We all have some melodies we need in order to live, to breathe, to be sustained, to continue on. All I have tried to do is give some reasons, sometimes oblique ones, for my particular tastes and the ways these sounds have led me to listen further to the surrounding world.

Sound *changes*. The moment you think you've caught it, it's gone. At last you learn how to take a dissonance to be an assonance, and then it moves somewhere else and you're no longer so sure. When listening to nature, you hear its contours, shapes, and edges—but what of the whole? While listening outward, you soon learn that the motion cannot be caught. There is always more to be heard.

Once in a while I hear something and sense that it's not quite enough and so I bend its end or beginning just a bit, and with the change it seems I need it and I belong to it and it repeats endlessly in my head and it won't go away and I am become the song and become the creator of one piece of a world I will own in a place it's clear I belong.

That's when you find you're an improviser, in the instant of sudden music. That's when the music finds its way out into nature. What a surprise to then know that it's been with us all along, that we have just forgotten how to hear it in the rain and the wind upon the trees, and to listen to what it says to us about how we ought to live.

CHANCE DESIGNS

Page 17, "Once in the mountains I came to a road which led up to a peak . . . ": Adapted from Vaslav Nijinsky, *Diary,* trans. and ed. Romola Nijinsky (London: Quartet Encounters, 1991).

Page 18, "Truth is, we may well be entering . . . ": Wallace Stevens, *Opus Posthumous* (New York: Vintage Books, 1990), 234.

Page 20, "Among all countries there is one country . . . ": this and all other Reb Nachman stories in this book are adapted from versions in Meyer Levin, *Classic Hassidic Tales* (1935; New York: Penguin Books, 1975).

ONE NOTE HISTORY

Page 27–28, "Long ago, a new kind of flute was invented in China . . . ": Stephen Nachmanovitch, *Free Play: Improvisation in Life and Art* (Los Angeles: Jeremy P. Tarcher, 1990), 1–3.

Page 34, "The key word in learning and playing the shakuhachi . . . ": Christopher Yohmei Blasdel, *The Shakuhachi: A Manual for Learning* (Tokyo: Ongaku no Tomo Sha, 1988), 66.

Page 35–36, "*Please tell me, what makes a good player . . .* ": "The Hitori Mondo of Hisamatsu Fuyo," trans. Robin Hartshorne and Kazuaki Tanahashi, *Annals of the International Shakuhachi Society* 1 (1984): 41– 45.

Page 40 – 42, Cases 75, 88, and 90 of the *Blue Cliff Record:* From David Rothenberg, *Blue Cliff Record: Zen Echoes* (New Paltz, N.Y.: Codhill Press, 2001).

Page 45, "It takes horseshit . . . ": From Stephen Berg's rather free version of Ikkyu, *Crow with No Mouth* (Port Townsend, Wash.: Copper Canyon Press, 1989), 47.

ROADS, MUSIC, RAPTURE

Page 61, on *saltanah:* Ali Jihad Racy, "Improvisation in Arab Music," in *In the Course of Performance: Studies in the World of Musical Improvisation,* ed. Bruno Nettl with Melinda Russell (Chicago: University of Chicago Press, 1999), 100.

THE SHADOW IS WHAT YOU HEAR

Page 69–70, "Auditory space has no favored focus . . . ": Edmund Carpenter, *Eskimo* (Toronto: University of Toronto Press, 1959), 26.

Page 71, "The echo is . . . ": Henry David Thoreau, "Sounds," *Walden* (1854; Boston: Beacon Press, 1997), 116.

Page 72, on the Bosavi: See Steven Feld, *Sound and Sentiment: Birds, Weeping, Poetics, and Song in Kaluli Expression,* 2d ed. (Philadelphia: University of Pennsylvania Press, 1990); and his CD, *Bosavi: Rainforest Music from Papua New Guinea,* Smithsonian Folkways 40487, 2001.

A SENSE OF SOUNDSCAPE

Page 87, "people and animals spoke the same language": Nalungiaq, "Magic Words," originally taken down in Danish by explorer Knud Rasmussen in 1927, turned into poetry by Edward Field, *Eskimo Songs and Stories* (New York: Delacorte Press, 1973), 7–8.

Page 91, "Over the woods this sound acquires . . . ": Thoreau, *Walden*, 116.

Page 98, "not to evoke landscape, but to *be* landscape": Brian Eno, quoted in *The Book of Music and Nature*, ed. David Rothenberg and Marta Ulvaeus (Middletown, Conn.: Wesleyan University Press, 2001), 239.

Page 102, "I heard the size of the ocean that night . . . ": Roger Payne, *Among Whales* (New York: Scribner, 1995), 145.

Page 102, Katy Payne on whales: Katherine Payne, "The Progressively Changing Songs of Humpback Whales: A Window on the Creative Process in a Wild Animal," in *The Origins of Music*, ed. Nils Wallin, Björn Merker, and Steven Brown (Cambridge, Mass.: MIT Press, 2001), 135–49.

Page 103, "Start off playing quietly . . . ": Jim Nollman, *The Charged Border: Where Whales and Humans Meet* (New York: Holt, 1999), 214, 66.

Page 103, on the Kwakiutl "song-maker": Edward S. Curtis, *The Kwakiutl*, vol. 10 of *The North American Indian* ([Seattle]: E. S. Curtis; [Cambridge, Mass.: The University Press], 1915), 171–72.

Page 105, on Adorno: This is what Frankfurt School theoretician Theodor Adorno, in exile in Los Angeles after fleeing the Nazis, had to say about jazz (writing in the 1950s): "Anyone who allows the growing respectability of mass culture to seduce him into equating a popular song with modern art because of a few false notes squeaked out by a clarinet; anyone who mistakes a triad studded with 'dirty notes' for atonality, has already capitulated to barbarism" ("Perennial Fashion—Jazz," in Theodor Adorno, *Prisms*, trans. Samuel Weber and Shierry Weber [Cambridge, Mass.: MIT Press, 1981], 127).

Page 105, "has brought us this far but then cast us out": A. R. Ammons, "For Harold Bloom," in *Selected Poems, 1951–1977* (New York: W. W. Norton, 1977), 105.

Page 108–9, "I narrowed the world down to the span of a few meters . . . ": Text adapted from E. O. Wilson, *Biophilia* (Cambridge, Mass.: Harvard University Press, 1984).

Page 109, "The love of complexity without reductionism makes art . . . ": E. O. Wilson, *Consilience: The Unity of Knowledge* (New York: Knopf, 1998), 54.

FOUR-FIFTHS OF THE WORLD CANNOT BE WRONG

Page 123, "She dances faster and faster . . . ": Ruth Holmes Whitehead, "The Child from beneath the Earth," in *Stories from the Six Worlds: Micmac Legends* (Halifax, Nova Scotia: Nimbus, 1988), 52.

Page 124, guns, germs, and steel: See Jared Diamond, *Guns, Germs, and Steel: The Fates of Human Societies* (New York: W. W. Norton, 1997).

Page 126, on Mr. Palomar: See Italo Calvino, *Mr. Palomar* (New York: Harcourt Brace, 1985), 3–8.

Page 139, "I'll tell you, in my way . . . ": The first two lines are from A. R. Ammons, *Glare* (New York: W. W. Norton, 1997).

THE THOUGHT AND THE STORY

Page 152, "And through the Tzaddik's *nigun* . . . ": Reb Nachman of Bratslav, "The Torah of the Void," trans. Zalman Shachter, in *A Big Jewish Book,* ed. Jerome Rothenberg (New York: Doubleday, 1978), 87.

Page 156, "There was a young mother who went to work in the fields . . . ": Laura Simms, in *Parabola* 24, no. 1 (1999): 102.

THE INSTRUMENT INCLUDES IT

Page 187, "consort with nature": Russell Sherman, *Piano Pieces* (New York: Farrar, Straus, Giroux, 1996), 3.

SOUND CHANGES

Page 195–96, "[weave] ideas from old facts . . . ": Wilson, *Consilience.*

Page 200, "Ditch your notated score . . . ": Evan Eisenberg, *The Ecology of Eden* (New York: Knopf, 1998), 293.

Nobody Could Explain It (Accurate Records AC 4004, 1991)

1. We Need Deserts
2. Thoreau Falls
3. Se Lo (trad. Tibetan)
4. Awake in Dreams
5. Song from Rettvik (trad. Swedish)
6. Nalungiaq
7. Wind of Design
8. Nigun of Ladi (trad. Hasidic)
9. The Last Day
10. Mani (trad. Tibetan)
11. Ras al Khaima.
12. Ellipsis . . .

13. Keeping Still

14. Three Sounds (Budapest, Hardanger, Home)

Graeme Boone	guitar
Hamid Drake	tabla, cymbals, Tibetan bowls
David Rothenberg	clarinets, keyboards, wind synthesizer, flutes, words
Dion Sorrell	electric cello

On the Cliffs of the Heart (Robi Droli/New Tone NT6744, 1995) with Graeme Boone and Glen Velez

1. In My Heart There Is a Discord (Guillaume de Machaut)
2. Man of Constant Sorrow (trad. Appalachian)
3. Prelude to the Dance of the Dervish (trad. Turkish)
4. Chikadedumpewaa
5. Joie Plaisence (Guillaume de Machaut)
6. Tales of the Big Drum
7. I See the Great Mountains (trad. Scottish)
8. Aux marches du palais (trad. French)
9. My Life with the Wave
10. Rai for Don
11. On the Cliffs of the Heart

Graeme Boone	banjo, guitar, vocals
David Rothenberg	clarinet, wind synthesizer
Glen Velez	frame drums, throat singing

Unamuno (Robi Droli/New Tone FY 7006, 1997)

1. Drums Stop
2. Toothwalking
3. Chernobyl/The Zone/7
4. Xarxa
5. Dakadoweàpaboom
6. 4 Joe Z

7. The Other

8. Berberia

9. Unamuno

10. Antarctica Melting

11. After Ikkyu

12. Whirr?

13. Accordion Crimes

14. Dry Forest (Booming, Buzzing)

15. By the Water's Edge

16. Pleas of Weddell Seals

Amit Chatterjee	guitar
Brahim Fribgane	frame drum
Abdul Outanen	oud
Douglas Quin	soundscapes
David Rothenberg	clarinet, keyboards, overtone flutes
Steve Scholle	shakuhachi
Chris Watson	soundscapes

Bangalore Wild (Wild Foundation WF9901, 1999)
with the Karnataka College of Percussion, featuring R. A. Ramamani

1. Raga Chakravakam

2. Raga Kuntala Varali

3. Raga Amrutha Varshini

4. Nalungiaq

5. Tlingit Song

6. Sa Re Ga

7. The End Is Not a Problem

8. Lament for the Vanishing, rehearsal

9. Lament for the Vanishing, concert

B. N. Chandramouli	kanjira
Gulraj	morsing
T. A. S. Mani	mridangam

Malini Mohan	violin
G. Omkar	konakkol (drum language)
R. A. Rajagopalan	ghatam
R. A. Ramamani	vocals, konakkol
David Rothenberg	clarinet, spoken word, prerecorded tapes
T. N. Shashikumar	tavil

Before the War (EarthEar ee9052, 2000)
with Douglas Quin

1. Beluga Siren
2. Murder in the World
3. Orchid Angels
4. Before the War
5. Karelian Midnight
6. Crabs Who Fall from the Trees into the Sea
7. Lines in the Sand
8. Swedish Folk Song #2
9. That's What Makes This World Dark
10. Kingfishing
11. Take Out the Loon!
12. Chirp Machine

Bill Douglass	bass, assorted flutes
Russ Gold	drums, percussion
Mari Järvinen	jouhikko, voice
Douglas Quin	field recordings, guitar, samplers, production
David Rothenberg	clarinets, words, keyboards

ACKNOWLEDGMENTS

Thanks to all my teachers in music over the years: Ken Fears, Armand Ambrosini, Paul McCandless, Brian Silver, Jimmy Giuffre, Joe Maneri, and especially the late Ivan Tcherepnin, to whom this book is dedicated. He's the first teacher I had who insisted that I follow no one's path but my own. Thanks too to all the musicians I've played with: Doug Stumberger, David Smith, Matthew Nathan, Dion Sorrell, Bendik Hofseth, Graeme Boone, John Rabinowitz, Marc Carnegie, Jeff Goldberg, Eugene Friesen, Hamid Drake, Glen Moore, Leon Gruenbaum, Amit Chatterjee, Jaron Lanier, Sussan Deihim, Richard Lerman, Douglas Quin, Bill Douglass, Russ Gold, Brahim Fribgane, Mark Brooks, Geoff Gersh, John Wieczorek, and Lisa Westberg, to name but a few.

Thanks to the Mesa Refuge for giving me a quiet place to finish this work, and to my agent, Kathleen Anderson, who worked so hard to get the publishing world interested. To those who have offered thoughts on the words inside my thanks as well: Evan Eisenberg, David Appelbaum, Debra Pughe, Jonathan Willard, Melissa Nelson, Oliver Lowenstein, Melita Rogelj, David Abram, Francisco Lopez, Chip Blake, Marta Ulvaeus, Jack Shoemaker, Joshua Glenn, and Rebecca Saletan, and to Barbara Ras for taking a chance on this wild and willful mix of sound and idea.

Portions of this work have appeared previously in different form in *Parabola, Terra Nova, Fourth Door Review, Orion,* and *The Best Spiritual Writing 1999,* edited by Philip Zaleski. Thanks to Mikael Levin for allowing me to quote liberally from his father Meyer Levin's book, *Classic Hasidic Tales.*

And I'd like to thank my parents, who always wished I would become a musician and nothing else; I hope I haven't disappointed them with the odd mix I have pursued. And thanks to my wife, Jaanika, and son, Jaan Umru, for listening and dancing along through all our days and nights together.

SUDDEN MUSIC: THE CD

1. Se Lo   8:02

   Geoff Gersh, cloud guitar
   David Rothenberg, clarinet
   John Wieczorek, percussion

   Monks of the Serlo Gompa Monastery, Jumbesi, Nepal, recorded
   November 1982.

2. Inclusive Gazes   5:44

   Robert Jürjendal, guitars and loops
   David Rothenberg, clarinet, bass clarinet, words
   Arvo Urb, drums and loops

   Recorded live at the Von Krahl Theatre Bar, in Tallinn, Estonia,
   January 2001.

   Text adapted from a tale by Reb Nachman of Bratslav.

3. Blue Cliff Cases   5:55

   Geoff Gersh, guitar
   David Rothenberg, clarinet, overtone flute, words
   Steve Scholle, shakuhachi
   John Wieczorek, percussion

   Text adapted from *The Blue Cliff Record,* a twelfth-century collection of
   Zen koans.

4. Exile   7:37

   David Rothenberg, frame drum, bass clarinet, synthesizer, words

   Ambient sounds of Helsinki recorded in December 2000 by Petri
   Kuljuntausta.

   Cuckoo and fly recorded in Endla Raba, Estonia, July 2000.

5. Night Train Shadow   5:22

   Geoff Gersh, cloud guitar
   David Rothenberg, clarinet

   Sounds of night insects and the midnight train recorded in the Cold Spring
   woods, August 2000.

6. White Crested Laughter   7:56

   Michael Pestel, flute
   David Rothenberg, clarinet
   White-Crested Laughing Thrush (*Garrulax leucolophus*), solo
   Nicobar Pigeon (*Caloenas nicobarica*), background coos
   Terry Lunsford, identification and encouragement

   Recorded live at the National Aviary, Pittsburgh, March 2001.

7. In the Rainforest   6:52

   David Rothenberg, keyboards, clarinet, words

   Text adapted from E. O. Wilson, *Biophilia.*

8. They Say   6:56

   Geoff Gersh, solo guitar
   Geetha Navale, veena
   Gopal Navale, rhythm guitar
   David Rothenberg, clarinet, Turkish clarinet, words
   Siddhartha, bass
   John Wieczorek, tabla

   Text adapted from the Upanishads, and more.

   Background loop recorded in Bangalore, October, 1998.

9. Crow on Snow   5:18

   David Rothenberg, keyboards, soprano saxophone, words

   Sounds of crows and other creatures recorded in Hall Quarry, Maine,
   August 1999.

10. Samchillian Duet   5:40

   Leon Gruenbaum, Samchillian Tip Tip Tip Cheeepeeeee
   David Rothenberg, clarinet

11. The Hundred Thousand Sounds (According to Our Study)   5:03

   Geoff Gersh, guitars
   John Wieczorek, percussion layers, laugh
   David Rothenberg, keyboard percussion, soprano saxophone, words

   Text adapted from Michael Kneissle, "Research into Changes in Brain
   Formation," *Newsletter of the Waldorf Steiner Kindergarten in Great Britain*
   (Spring/Summer 1999).

   Thanks to Casey Walker for alerting me to the findings of this study.

TOTAL TIME: 70:50

All titles published by Mysterious Mountain Music (BMI)
© ℗ *David Rothenberg 2002*

All pieces recorded at Storm King Sound, Cold Spring, N.Y., unless otherwise noted.

Philosopher and musician David Rothenberg is the author of *Hand's End: Technology and the Limits of Nature* (California, 1993) and *Blue Cliff Record: Zen Echoes* (Lindisfarne, 2000). He is the founding editor of the Terra Nova book series, which includes *The Book of Music and Nature* (Wesleyan, 2001) and *Writing on Water* (MIT Press, 2001). His writing has appeared in *Parabola, The Nation, Wired, Dwell,* and *Sierra.* An associate professor of philosophy at the New Jersey Institute of Technology, Rothenberg speaks and performs all over the world, and he has released five CDs, the most recent being *Before the War* (EarthEar, 2000). He lives in Cold Spring, New York.